TENNIS
The Skills of the Game

TENNIS
The Skills of the Game

CHARLES APPLEWHAITE
and BILL MOSS

The Lawn Tennis Association

THE CROWOOD PRESS

First published in 1987 by
THE CROWOOD PRESS
Ramsbury, Marlborough
Wiltshire SN8 2HE

Paperback edition 1988

British Library Cataloguing in Publication Data

Moss, Bill
   Tennis: The Skills of the Game
   1. Tennis
   I. Title   II. Applewhaite, Charles
   769.342'2   GV995

   ISBN 0 946284 99 7 (HB)
        1 85223 124 6 (PB)

Acknowledgements

Demonstration photographs by Peter Richardson; action
photographs by Tommy Hindley.
Figs 8 to 13, 21, 25, 27, 30 and 33 by Luigi Stefanelli; all other line
illustrations by Vanetta Joffe.

The authors thank Bev Risman for his contribution to The Physical
Game.

Series advisor David Bunker, Lecturer, Loughborough University
of Technology.

Throughout this book the pronouns 'he', 'him' and 'his' have been
used inclusively, and are intended to apply to both men and
women. It is important in sport, as elsewhere, that women and men
should have equal status and equal opportunities.

Typeset by Q-Set, Gloucester
Printed in Great Britain at The University Printing House, Oxford

Contents

Charles Applewhaite is Director of Coaching for The Lawn Tennis Association. He has been involved in tennis for over thirty years, winning the Junior Doubles at Wimbledon, and playing in the senior Singles, Doubles and Mixed Doubles between 1958 and 1965. He has represented England in the Home Internationals, won the British Professional Singles and Doubles titles on several occasions, and played Team Tennis in Germany. He qualified as a professional coach in 1965, was appointed LTA Regional Coach in 1969, and became National Coach/Development Officer in the North West in 1982 before taking up his current appointment in 1985.

Bill Moss is National Coach/Consultant to The Scottish Lawn Tennis Association, and President of the Professional Tennis Coaches' Association. During a distinguished career, he won the British Professional Championships three times and was British Professional Doubles Champion eighteen times, as well as being European Professional Doubles Champion with Fred Perry. He was coach to Warwickshire from 1950 to 1961 and National Coach to Scotland from 1962 to 1982. Since his retirement from competitive tennis he has concentrated on the development of coaching, and has been instrumental in restructuring the LTA coaching syllabus.

There have been many books written for the tennis enthusiast which are read avidly and then put aside. Now, in this publication, all players have a golden opportunity to acquire knowledge and to retain it, by keeping this excellently presented reference book to hand.

Tennis in Britain is beginning to attract larger numbers of players, and these beginners are in need of advice and guidance on how to improve their game. Whatever your level of play, whether beginner, advanced player or coach, this book outlines the many different ways to improve your standard.

Sue Mappin
National Women's Team Manager

I have known Bill Moss and Charles Applewhaite for many years, both as players and coaches. They have always, in their coaching, understood the players' needs, and their book reflects this. It is more than just a technical book that identifies strokes and the way to play them; it presents all the different facets of tennis in a clear and concise manner.

Whatever standard of player you are or wish to be, this book will help you to achieve a better understanding of the game of tennis.

Dan Maskell, CBE

Introduction

Welcome to the skills of tennis! This book looks at the game of tennis from the starter and recreational levels right up to that of the committed tennis player who wants to improve his performance, whether in the area of technique, tactics, psychology, fitness or match play. Even experienced tennis players should find the first section on basic skills and strokes of interest, if only to reaffirm their previous understanding of the principles of hitting effective shots. Conversely, the inexperienced player should enjoy reading and attempting on court some of the more advanced skills. The instructions given refer to right-handed players; left-handed players should read left for right and vice versa.

Tennis can be a game of power or of subtle stroke play, offering many opportunities of achieving a successful result. Only by learning and understanding the game's many skills can you become a truly efficient player. This will demand time and practice, but perfecting your game can also be fun. You will need:

1. To develop a sound basic technique, leading to advanced stroke production.
2. To develop a tactical awareness that will allow you to use your racket skills to best advantage.
3. To develop the will and the determination to improve and become a winner.
4. To maintain a level of fitness at all times.
5. To remember that the fun and enjoyment of playing should always be a strong element, no matter what level of play you achieve.

All tennis players who originally took to the courts for the pure enjoyment of the game will, on graduating to a friendly singles match, have found something in common with a player in the more serious arena of Wimbledon. They are facing competition and trying to win. It is from this common denominator that players try to improve their game.

We hope that this book will stimulate readers of all ages to go out, practise and play this marvellous and enjoyable game. We challenge you to read on and improve your tennis.

1 Basic Skills

This chapter will cover the fundamentals of tennis strokes and provide the foundation for developing the more sophisticated skills that are necessary to become a better player. Remember the fundamentals apply to you just as they do to the Wimbledon champions.

To play an effective game of tennis you must have a good understanding of the basic skills. These are:

1. Ball sense and movement.
2. Hitting area and contact point.
3. Use of the racket head.
4. The linked fundamentals.
5. Ready position.

BALL SENSE

The primary skill required is ball sense. As a player this means you must learn not only to watch the ball as you are hitting it but also, most importantly, to watch the ball as your opponent is hitting it. From what you see and the information you have gathered you must make decisions as to where the ball is going, at what speed and where it is likely to bounce. All this seems fairly simple. The most difficult aspect is to respond to the information, particularly for the beginner who experiences great difficulty in getting to the right place at the right time. Remember that you are dealing with a moving ball, put into your half of the court

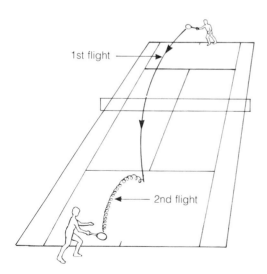

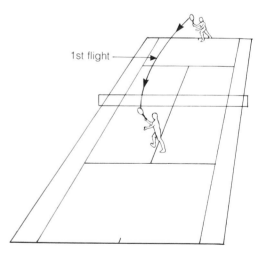

Fig 1 *The ball has two flights when groundstrokes are played; one when it is volleyed or smashed.*

by an opponent who intends to make it as difficult as possible for you to play it back into his half of the court. It is all about cues and responses.

Tennis demands a highly developed ball sense. You must be able to respond to the speed, flight, direction and the bounce of the ball. Concentration and alertness will help you to anticipate your opponent's play, and your positioning on court is also important.

Tennis is a two and one flight game: the ball has two flights when forehand and backhand groundstrokes are played and one when the ball is volleyed and smashed.

HITTING AREA/ CONTACT POINT

The next basic skill is the ability to apply ball sense to develop a sound and regular method of hitting the ball through correct positioning. In order to do this successfully, each type of stroke should be played using the same movement pattern. This ensures that the ball appears in the same place in relation to the body each and every time.

By establishing this hitting area or contact point the player is able to develop a grooved (consistent) method, and if the contact point is regularly maintained it becomes more simple to adjust the direction and control of the shot.

Groundstrokes (*Figs 2 to 4*)

The hitting area and contact point cover three dimensions:

1. The ball should be struck at a height somewhere between knee and waist height. This is physically the most natural level for playing groundstrokes.
2. The ball should be struck at the side and slightly in front of the body.
3. The ball should be struck at a comfortable distance from the body.

Beginners will find it easier to hit the ball after the top of the bounce, but should *not* be discouraged from playing the ball before this point.

Planning a sound position for striking the ball around the three dimensions will emphasise the following points:

(a)   (b)   (c)

Fig 2   Hitting area: forehand.

|(a)|(b)|(c)|

Fig 3 Hitting area: single-handed backhand.

|(a)|(b)|(c)|

Fig 4 Hitting area: two-handed backhand.

1. You will need to watch the ball more carefully.

2. You will have more time to produce your shot.

3. You will develop a more methodical positioning to the ball.

4. The arc of the falling ball from the top of the bounce tends to encourage a correct path of the forward swing of the racket.

5. You will develop better balance.

6. You will have better control and more power in stroke production.

Service (*Fig 5*)

In a game, the only time you are stationary is when you are serving. This is also the only time that you are in control of all the action taking place. It is important that you make the most of this stroke opportunity, and the placement of the ball is crucial.

The hitting area and contact point again cover three dimensions:

1. The ball should be struck at approxi-

(a)   (b)   (c)

Fig 5   Hitting area: service.

mately maximum hitting height.
2.   The ball should be struck slightly forward of the body and towards the target.
3.   The ball should be struck slightly to the right-hand side of the body.

You should practise all three dimensions of ball placement. When they work as one unit within the whole action of the service you will have achieved the basic hitting position of the service.

Planning a sound position for striking the ball around the three dimensions will help you to develop:

1.   A more methodical approach.
2.   A grooved stroke.
3.   A more natural throwing action.
4.   Better control and direction.
5.   Better balance.
6.   More power.

Volleys *(Figs 6 & 7)*

For this stroke you are much closer to your opponent when he is hitting the ball into your half of the court. This means that you need quicker responses to get into a sound position from which to volley.

The hitting area and contact point now only cover two dimensions:

1.   The ball should be struck in front of the body.
2.   The ball should be struck slightly to the side of the body, but nearer to the body than for groundstrokes.

Planning a sound position for striking the ball around the two dimensions will help you to develop:

1.   A more methodical shot.
2.   A grooved shot.

(a)

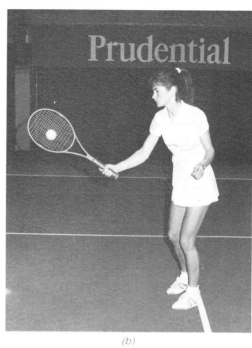
(b)

Fig 6   Hitting area: forehand volley.

(a)

(b)

Fig 7   Hitting area: backhand volley.

3. A firmer shot.
4. Better balance.
5. Better control and power.

Summary

Remember, you must make maximum use of your ball sense to respond to the flight of the ball and position yourself to the ball in such a way that you can hit it with a smooth, rhythmical action. It is important to study and practise the hitting areas and contact points covering groundstrokes, serves and volleys if you want to progress. It sounds very simple, but it needs a lot of practice.

USE OF THE RACKET HEAD

You now know how to relate yourself to the ball for all your shots and will be regularly taking up the right position at the right time to perform the simple task of hitting the ball. To hit the ball back into your opponent's half of the court you must have a sound, simple racket skill, which must also be grooved and consistent. The following are the essential differences in the use of the racket head:

Groundstrokes Swing the racket head.
Service Throw the racket head.
Volley Punch or block the racket head.

Groundstrokes (*Figs 8 to 10*)

1. Early preparation – give yourself the maximum time and use a smooth take-back.
2. The falling ball from the top of the bounce encourages the correct path of the racket head.
3. Effective swing of the racket head is

only achieved by having a good hitting area and contact point.
4. Use a swinging racket action.

All these points apply whether you use one hand or two for a particular shot.

If you let your eyes follow the path of the racket head from backswing to follow-through a number of times, you can begin to feel the swinging action of the racket head.

Service (*Fig 11*)

1. Adopt a comfortable but strong throwing stance.
2. To achieve the correct head movement, the ball placement must be towards the target, in front and slightly to the racket side of the body, and at an effective hitting height.
3. Develop an explosive position of the racket behind the head.
4. Use a throwing action of the racket at the ball.

By following the path of the racket head from backswing to follow-through, you should be able to see this throwing action.

Volleys (*Figs 12 & 13*)

1. You are now closer to your opponent and will have less time to prepare than for the groundstrokes.
2. Make contact with the ball only slightly to the side but always in front of the body.
3. Keep firm control of the racket; little backswing is required.
4. Use a short blocking or punching action.

(a)

(b)

(c)

(d)

Fig 8   Forehand drive.

(a)

(b)

(c)

(d)

Fig 9   Backhand drive.

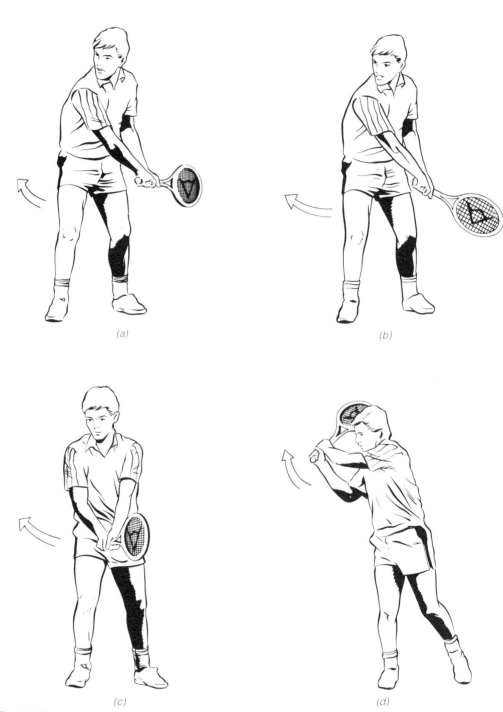

(a)

(b)

(c)

(d)

Fig 10   Two-handed backhand drive.

(a)

(b)

(c)

(d)

ig 11   Service.

(a)

(b)

(c)

(d)

Fig 12   Forehand volley.

(a)

(b)

(c)

(d)

Fig 13   Backhand volley.

Summary

You may find that your major problem in the use of the racket head is that you tend to develop too much power and have too little control. It is important that in the early stages you hit the ball in a controlled manner, with a firm contact (even if only very softly) and not necessarily using the full court area.

Remember, using the racket head correctly needs controlled practice.

THE LINKED FUNDAMENTALS

It is important that now you have laid the foundation of becoming a more efficient player – by thinking of quality of movement, positioning for hitting the ball and the use of the racket head – you work at the linked fundamentals that are the basis of sound stroke play.

The following fundamentals have an important role in developing quality stroke play formed from the basic skills:

1. Watching the ball.
2. Footwork.
3. Balance.
4. Control of the racket swing, throw and punch.
5. Control of the racket face.

Watching the Ball

Everybody watches the ball when they play tennis, but the good player watches it more carefully and reacts more precisely than the average player. If you want to improve this aspect of your game, try looking as soon as your opponent has hit the ball at:

1. The trajectory of the shot.
2. The probable landing place of the ball
3. The place you will need to move to in order to play a comfortable shot.
4. Any spin on the ball that might affect your previous observations.

Your brain should be sifting all this information to enable you to achieve your objective. This aspect of the game requires tremendous concentration and application if you wish to raise your technical skills to a higher level.

Footwork

Tennis is a game of explosive movement. Your half of the single court only measures 39 × 27 feet (11.88 × 8.23 metres) which does not appear to be a very large area to cover. However, it generally takes only two to three seconds for a ball hit by your opponent to reach or pass you, so you often have very little time in which to play your shot. Good, quick footwork is therefore essential.

In tennis there are two major types of footwork:

1. The movement to the ball, which must generally be fast and explosive, enabling you to reach the ball in good time for your shot.
2. The small adjusting footwork when you reach the ball. This will enable you to set yourself up to the ball well and play the shot in your favourite hitting area and with your best method.

Whenever you watch a good player, instead of watching the play and the ball, try just looking at the player. Notice how he reacts as his opponent hits the ball. You will pick up his fast explosive movements to cover the distance and his final adjustments prior to the shot. This should give you a good idea of the different levels of footwork required.

Good players make any sport seem easy but most of their hard work goes unseen, especially their footwork. Try studying it.

Balance

Balance plays an important role in all sports, and tennis is no exception. There are two major areas of balance to consider:

1. The balancing position at the end of a movement prior to the hit.
2. The balance required during the hit.

When you move very quickly from one position to another and then slow down or stop quickly, there is always a possibility of losing balance. As this is the moment in tennis when you will be about to play your shot, it is very important that you develop the art of moving quickly to the ball and then retaining a balanced position prior to the shot.

However, there is still fifty per cent of the work to be done, as it is fundamental to the success of the shot that as you begin to swing the racket you retain your balance in order to control the swing and direction of the shot. If you lose balance just as you are about to make contact with the ball, the result will probably be an uncontrolled shot.

Tennis is a game of controlled balance. Practise controlling yours.

Control of Racket Movement

The previous fundamentals are very specific in assisting you to reach the ball and set yourself up for the shot. You are now ready to move the racket in the most efficient way

to hit the ball. You will need to think in terms of the speed of swing, angle of swing and overall shape of the swing. It will help if you visualise the racket as a natural extension of the arm.

There are two distinct phases to a swing. The first is the controlled backswing, which should prepare you well for the second and most important phase, the hitting or forward swing. These phases should be linked together in a rhythmical and efficient manner to achieve a successful shot.

There are many different shots and therefore many different movement patterns for the racket (swing, throw, punch), so before the racket movement can be controlled it is necessary to have a clear mental picture of the shot being attempted. There are major differences, for example, between a forehand volley and a backhand lob. The first is a short, sharp, fast, generally downwards movement; the second is a slow, long upward swing. To be successful you need a good understanding of the type of movement you are trying to achieve, and you should try to follow your mental picture of the particular movement patterns for each shot.

Try watching good players and notice how they manage to play a consistent controlled swing on a particular shot. Now practise yours!

Control of Racket Face

All the fundamentals have been leading up to this, the most important time in any ball game – contact with the ball. This moment will decide whether or not the ball is going into play. The ball is only in contact with the racket for three milliseconds, so the contact must be set up exactly the first time. The moment the ball is struck, the angle created by the racket face at impact point will determine where the ball will bounce. There are no second chances.

A particular method of holding the racket for each shot (i.e. the grip) should be selected early, and any grip change should be accomplished in the early parts of the backswing.

The racket face must be firmly controlled during the preparation swing prior to impact, as this will facilitate racket face control at the most important time – contact.

At contact point the racket should be held with a firm but flexible grip, with the racket face angled towards the target. Try to visualise the racket as a rifle and the ball as the bullet. The moment when you pull the trigger (contact point) the rifle (racket) should be aiming directly towards the target. If you accomplish this, the ball should reach its target – the court. There is no magic about it if you practise it regularly.

Summary

The linked fundamentals are similar to a chain: it is only as strong as its weakest link. If your chain has a weak link, locate it and try to strengthen it by regular practice. However, do not fall into the trap of only practising the weaknesses. Good players are the ones with strengths, so make sure you also work at your strengths. Putting the two together will provide you with the basis of sound stroke production that you can depend upon in match play.

READY POSITION

Whether you are working at groundstrokes, service or volley, you must start from a position of readiness.

Groundstrokes (*Fig 14*)

1. Relaxed position.
2. Feet shoulder width apart, body bent over towards the racket head with the knees slightly bent.
3. Eyes focused on opponent, concentrating completely.
4. Roughly 3 to 4 feet (a metre) behind the baseline when playing from the back of the court.
5. A good player will support the racket with the free hand prior to receiving service and also between strokes.

Service (*Fig 15*)

1. Comfortable sideways position.
2. A strong throwing stance.
3. Both feet must be behind the baseline
4. Feet about shoulder width apart.
5. Hands pointing towards the target.
6. Ball and racket together at the beginning of the movement.

Volley (*Fig 16*)

Remember that for this stroke you are much nearer your opponent.

1. Alert springy position, with the racket supported at the throat or neck by the spare hand and held above the height of the net.
2. Feet shoulder width apart, body bent over towards the target with the knees slightly bent.
3. Eyes focused on opponent.
4. Roughly 7 to 8 feet (2 metres) from the net near the centre service line.

(a)   (b)

Fig 14   Groundstroke ready position.

(a)   (b)   (c)

Fig 15   Service ready position.

(a)

(b)

Fig 16   Volley ready position.

SHORT (MINI) TENNIS

For many players, especially the very young, their first attempts at tennis are often highly dissatisfying, and it does not appear to be the same game that the tennis stars play. The reason for this is that the very young tennis player often finds the court too big, the net too high, the racket too heavy and the tennis balls uncontrollable. This results in frustration, lack of success, boredom and, most importantly, no fun for the young participant. Such players should be encouraged to start with short tennis.

Short tennis is a proportionally reduced game with a smaller court, lower net, plastic bat and a soft, sponge ball, which has dramatically changed the game of tennis for young starters. Because the court areas are now in relation to the size of the player and the ball bounces more slowly,

Fig 17   Young players can benefit from starting with short tennis.

young players can play successfully using the basic skills of tennis, with long rallies and a great deal of movement, mimicking all the shots that the top stars play in their major competitions.

The most important thing, however, is that the players will have an enormous amount of fun. Short tennis thus provides tremendous stimulation for young starters to develop the basic skills of tennis, making it a direct and early preparation for the real game.

The Court *(Fig 18)*

The court area is approximately a quarter of the size of a normal tennis court. A short tennis court can be put on to a standard badminton court by reducing the height of the net to 2 feet 7 inches (80cm) and using the outside badminton lines as external measurements.

The Bat and Ball

Short tennis bats are made of plastic and are just over half the size of a normal tennis racket. The ball is made of soft, absorbent foam which has the effect of slowing the ball in the air and reducing its bounce. It is therefore easy to keep it in play.

Basic Rules

1. The best of three games constitutes a match.
2. The game is played up to eleven points. If the score reaches ten all, two

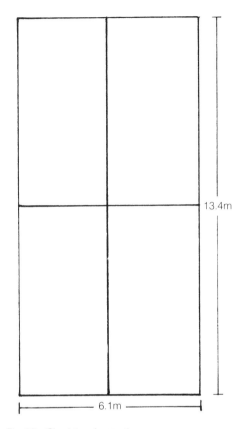

Fig 18   Short tennis court.

clear points are played.
3. The service changes hands every two points, the server having two attempts to place the ball into court.
4. The service from the right-hand court should be placed in the opponent's left-hand court (as viewed from the server).
5. The normal rules of tennis are enforced.

2 Basic Strokes

Having explored the basic skills, we will now look in detail at the technical skills required to hit basic strokes efficiently. What are basic strokes? In this instance, we are referring to those shots hit with the minimum amount of spin, commonly known as the 'bread and butter' shots of most tennis players. Some players who regularly play heavy topspin or slice will consider these to be their 'bread and butter' strokes. However, we are covering spin in Chapter 3 so for the sake of clarity, basic strokes here are those hit either flat or with very little spin.

Although you are working primarily on *stroke play*, try to remember the fundamentals:

1. Get to the ball poised and well balanced.
2. Take up a good position for striking the ball.
3. Use the racket head correctly.

It is important at this stage, before studying in detail the basic technical skills and advanced skills, to understand why you use them.

In match play you must be able to play different roles at any given time. These are your roles when in defence, when attacking, and when counter-attacking. These roles and the success you make of them will depend on your range of technical skills controlled by the following factors:

1. Your own planning and shot selection when you are able to dictate the play.

2. Your ability and sound stroke play when your opponent is dictating the play.

To be strong in all three roles, you must have a sound technique supported by advanced racket skills, and understand how the use of spin can play a major role. Not only should you practise hard at developing a sound technique and advanced racket skills, but you should remember that the purpose of these skills is to enable you to put the ball into play consistently and win the point and, ultimately, the match.

The same applies to top class players. They generally stay well in control of the situation and the principles of sound stroke production. These have been practised over a long period of time and remain secure even in the most difficult pressure situations. *Fig 19* shows a situation that happens continually in high level play: a player moving for a wide ball. Notice:

1. She is retaining balance and poise.
2. The racket is well under control while moving.
3. She is striving for the best possible hitting position.
4. She has a determined approach, playing the best possible shot and maintaining quality under pressure.

Fig 19 Virginia Wade preparing for a wide backhand.

FOREHAND DRIVE

Individual interpretation becomes an important factor in how a player will eventually play a shot, and the major influence will be the grip. *Fig 20* clearly shows a different approach to the forehand. A Western grip and a stance which is much more open and closer to the ball – these characteristics add up to a formidable forehand. This is the basic Becker forehand played with a heavy topspin. The variations he uses from this forehand are to hit with less topspin or to slice the shot.

As a player, you could have a variation of grip anywhere between the Eastern and the Western grip. If you favour the Western,

remember that you will have the ball a little closer to the body and your stance will be more open. If you are in doubt as to which grip to use, stick with the basic Eastern as it is the simpler method to follow.

Eastern or Shake Hands Grip
(*Fig 21*)

Points

1. Palm behind the handle.
2. Natural extension of the hand.
3. Maximum strength achieved this way.
4. Easy to hit effectively balls of varying height.

21

Fig 20   Boris Becker plays a forehand with a heavy topspin.

Fig 21   Eastern grip.

Method (*Fig 22*)

1.   Start from the ready position.
2.   Take the racket back early.
3.   Make a smooth connection between backswing and forward swing.
4.   Prepare on the right foot; step in with the left foot.
5.   Hit through the ball, striking it when it is about level with the leading hip, at a comfortable distance from the body and at a comfortable height.
6.   On completion of the stroke, the racket finishes level with the head, and the upper body finishes facing the net.
7.   Maintain balance.
8.   Return to the ready position.

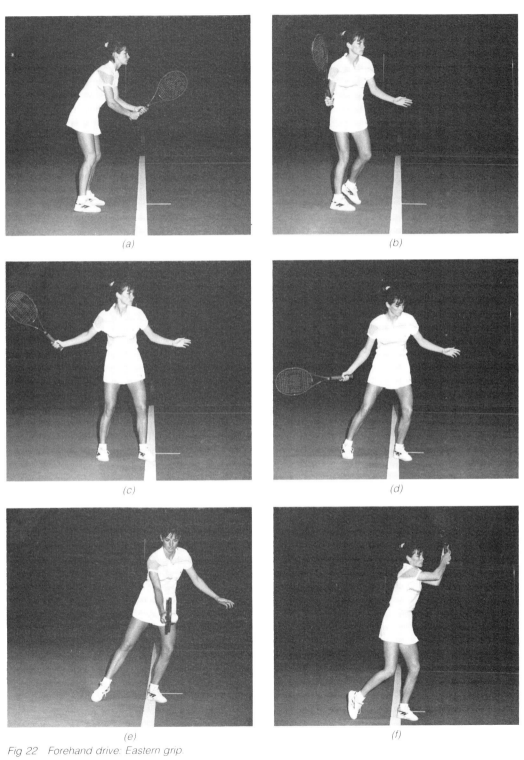

(a)

(b)

(c)

(d)

(e)

(f)

Fig 22   Forehand drive: Eastern grip.

23

(a)

(b)

(c)

(d)

(e)

(f)

Fig 23   Forehand drive: Western grip

Western Grip *(Fig 24)*

Points

1. Palm underneath handle.
2. Natural position for hitting balls above waist height (high bouncers).
3. Facilitates a stronger hit on high shots.
4. Leads into the use of topspin.

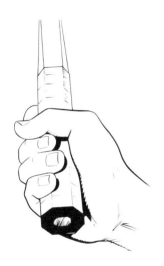

Fig 24   Western grip.

Method (Fig 23)

1. Start from the ready position.
2. Take the racket back early.
3. Make a smooth connection between backswing and forward swing.
4. Prepare on the right foot. Keep stance open, with body weight forward at impact.
5. Hit through the ball, striking it when it is about level with the leading hip, at a comfortable distance from the body, and at a comfortable height.
6. At impact the arm should be less extended and the ball should be played closer to the body than in the Eastern forehand grip.
7. Good wrist action is essential because of the closed racket face.
8. On completion of the stroke, the racket finishes level with the head, and the upper body finishes facing the net.

SINGLE-HANDED BACKHAND DRIVE

Grip *(Fig 26)*

The grip is obtained by taking an Eastern forehand grip and turning the hand inwards a quarter of a turn, with the thumb diagonally across the back of the handle. The hand is now more on top of the racket.

Points

1. Greater strength behind the handle.
2. Flexibility, encouraging a variety of shots.
3. A sensitive as well as a strong grip.
4. Encourages all-round racket face control.

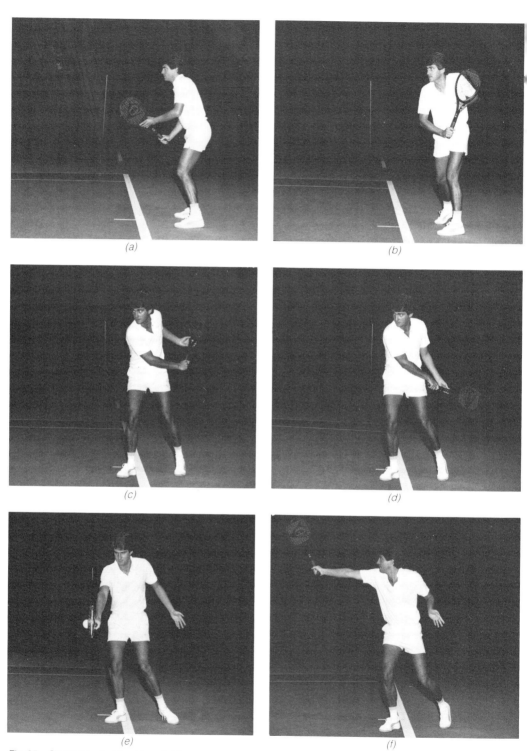

(a)

(b)

(c)

(d)

(e)

(f)

Fig 25   Single-handed backhand drive.

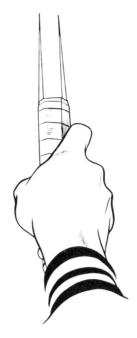

Fig 26 Grip for single-handed backhand drive.

Method (*Fig 25*)

1. Start from the ready position.
2. Take the racket back early.
3. Change the grip as the body turns away. More body turn is necessary than for the forehand drive. The back of the hitting shoulder is towards the net at the end of the backswing.
4. Make a smooth connection between backswing and forward swing, using the free hand to support the racket at the throat during the backswing.
5. Prepare on the left leg. Step in and across with the right leg, putting the foot down before the ball is struck. Keep the knees bent.
6. Hit through the ball when it is slightly in front of the leading hip at a comfortable distance from the body.
7. Develop lift in the forward swing; swing low to high.
8. Racket finishes head high, with the upper body facing the net at the completion of the stroke.
9. Maintain balance throughout the shot.

TWO-HANDED BACKHAND DRIVE

Grip (*Fig 29*)

The right hand takes a single-handed backhand grip. The left hand takes an Eastern forehand grip. The hands are close together.

Points

1. Increased strength.
2. Increased racket face control.
3. Possible extra power and speed of swing.
4. Increased flexibility and disguise on shots.

(a)

(b)

(c)

(d)

(e)

(f)

Fig 27   Two-handed backhand drive, keeping both hands on racket.

| (a) | (b) |

Fig 28 Alternatively, the top hand can be released after contact with the ball.

Fig 29 Grip for two-handed backhand drive.

Method (*Figs 27 & 28*)

1. Effectiveness of the stroke derives from sound grips.
2. Early preparation is important because both hands must be brought together on the racket handle in good time to play a shot.
3. You need to get closer to the ball, owing to restricted reach.
4. Not so much shoulder turn prior to shot as with single-handed backhand.
5. Even more stress on stepping forward into the shot. Prepare on the left foot and step into the shot on the right foot.
6. There are two basic methods of playing this stroke: keeping two hands on the racket throughout the stroke, or releasing with the top hand after making contact with the ball.
7. There are many successful variations of this stroke.

Backhand Summary

Early attempts to develop a sound backhand often use the common escape route of running round the backhand to play the

29

stronger forehand skills, but this delays the improvement of backhand play. Don't use escape routes, settle for developing a sound basic backhand.

For many players, however, the burning question is should I use one or two hands? If you are not yet certain which method to use, study the advantages and disadvantages of both and experiment until you are ready to develop a particular method. Once you have decided on one method, however, do try to persevere with it and make it as effective and reliable as you possibly can.

TWO-FISTED GRIP (Fig 30)

Before leaving the single-handed and two-handed play of groundstrokes, it is important to consider a unique method of two-handed play. If you favour this method, you will surely play in similar fashion to its

greatest exponent Jimmy Connors. *Fig 3* clearly shows the aggressive two-fiste grip: two strong forehands, with both wrist very firm and the racket taken back almo at the same height as the bounce of th ball. The racket face is square to the ba and that is how impact is made. It cor tinues that way through the ball giving th appearance of a very flat trajectory wit very little or no topspin. In many instance the ball is played powerfully with sligh slice.

Remember, this method is one aggression, where attacking the rising ba is the name of the game.

Fig 31   Jimmy Connors plays with an aggressive two-fisted grip.

Fig 30   Two-fisted grip.

LOBS *(Fig 32)*

Forehand and backhand lobs are within groundstroke play and should closely follow the pattern of all the basic forehand and backhand drives. The grips are the same as for the drives.

Points

1. A stroke with a strong defensive quality.
2. A stroke to break up the play of the aggressive net player.
3. A stroke that can turn defence into attack.

(a)   (b)   (c)

(d)   (e)   (f)

Fig 32   Backhand lob.

Method

1. Early preparation.
2. Low backswing.
3. Steep lifting motion – very low to very high.
4. Smooth, slow, controlled swing.
5. Open racket face at impact.
6. Firm wrist on impact.
7. High follow-through.
8. Maintain balance.

SERVICE

The service starts play; nothing can happen until the service is delivered. Its importance to the rest of your game is crucial – the confidence it generates should not be underestimated. The time and effort you put into perfecting a sound technique will bring their rewards. The true strength of your serving ability will depend on all-round safe methods for first and second services.

You will see more individual interpretations of service than almost any other stroke in the game, but, whatever style you finally settle on, it should contain sound basics and those fundamentals we explored earlier.

Keep the action simple – place the ball in the air with one hand, throw the racket face at it with the other.

The Chopper (Service) Grip *(Fig 33)*

This grip is somewhere between the basic Eastern forehand and basic Eastern backhand grips. Beginners may find it easier to start with a forehand grip and adjust by degrees as skill develops. The advantages of the chopper grip are that it:

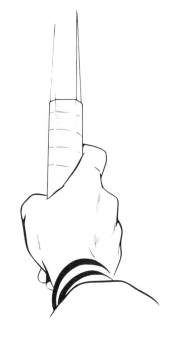

Fig 33   Chopper (service) grip.

1. Gives more flexibility.
2. Encourages greater racket head speed.
3. Assists the use of controlled spin.
4. Encourages the use of service variation.

Method *(Fig 34)*

1. Adopt a sideways position of readiness, in a comfortable but strong throwing stance.
2. Both eyes look straight at the target.
3. The ball and racket hands start together to produce a rhythmical beginning.
4. Place the ball accurately in the air, just above full hitting height and slightly in front of the body.

5. The racket should be in an explosive throwing position behind the head.
6. Stretch upwards for maximum hitting height.

7. Body weight follows the direction of the ball.
8. Retain balance throughout the action.

(a)   (b)   (c)

(d)   (e)   (f)

Fig 34 Service.

VOLLEYS

Before studying the techniques it is worth considering the following points:

1. The distance between yourself and your opponent on the baseline is very much reduced; things will happen faster so you must be very alert. You must adopt a ready position from which you can move quickly to the ball.
2. There is now only one flight of the ball to contend with, so quick thinking and quick reactions are essential.

The Grip

The volley grip is the same as that for the basic groundstrokes: the Eastern forehand for the forehand volley; the Eastern backhand grip for the backhand volley. As you develop the basic volley action and confidence you can refine and adjust the grips. To save time in changing grips and to give

(a)

(b)

(c)

(d)

Fig 35 Forehand volley

(a) (b)

(c) (d)

Fig 36   Single-handed backhand volley.

increased flexibility, you may well choose a volley grip that is half-way between your own personal forehand and backhand grips.

Method (*Figs 35 to 37*)

1.   Start from the ready position.
2.   Short backswing of the racket.
3.   The volley is played at the side and slightly in front of the body (the hitting area/contact point).
4.   The emphasis is on blocking or punching with the racket head.

5.   Correct use of the racket head.
6.   Keep firm control of the racket throughout.
7.   Short follow-through.
8.   Maintain balance throughout; put your weight into the shot.
9.   A quick recovery is necessary for next shot.

(a)

(b)

(c)

(d)

Fig 37   Two-handed backhand volley.

SMASH

Your net play will never be secure until you have mastered what is possibly the most dynamic shot in the game, the smash. It is probably the most under-practised stroke in the game of tennis by the average player, mainly because of its degree of difficulty in relation to the movement required to get back underneath the lob. *Backwards* – that's the key to good smashing. How do you move backwards quickly, poised and well balanced? The answer is sideways.

The smash is an extension of the service except that your opponent has placed (badly) the ball in the air and you have to move well to set up a serving position.

The Grip

Use the chopper (service) grip; although less able players may find it easier to begin with a forehand grip and adjust by degrees as skill develops.

(a) (b)

(c) (d)

Fig 38 Smash.

Method (*Fig 38*)

1. Move back from the volley position in *sideways* steps as soon as you can see the lob from your opponent.
2. Take your racket back into the throwing position early, using a shortened back-swing.
3. Take a longer last stride just before throwing the racket head at the ball, using the non-hitting hand to assist correct alignment on the ball (correct hitting area/ contact point).
4. Put your weight into the smash, reach up to meet the ball and strike it at your maximum reaching height.
5. Recover to a ready position.

3 Strokes with Spin

SPINS

Correct usage of spin is a vital requirement of basic and advanced stroke play. Even when practising the simple use of the racket head swing, throw and punch suggested earlier you will have been putting spin on the ball – in many instances unintentionally. You will certainly have experienced how disconcerting it can be to play a shot against a ball that is spinning severely:

1. It upsets your footwork when you believe you have positioned yourself well.
2. It upsets the rhythm of your swing.
3. It upsets your timing, causing you to mishit shots.
4. If your opponent varies his spin it can upset your game as you cannot settle down into a grooved rhythm. You can equally upset your opponent's stroke play by imparting spin on the ball intentionally.

Using spin will enhance your effectiveness as a player, so we will now look at the basic spins you will use.

Types of Spin (Fig 39)

Topspin

If, after hitting it, the ball is revolving towards your opponent, you will have hit the ball with topspin.

The simple effect of topspin on a ball which has not yet bounced is that it will tend to come down quickly. The effect of topspin on a ball after the bounce is that it will travel towards your opponent quickly with a fairly high bounce.

Slice

If, after hitting it, the ball is revolving towards you (although travelling towards your opponent), you will have hit the ball with slice.

The simple effect of slice on a ball travelling through the air is that it will tend to stay in the air longer. After the bounce, the effect will be for it to have a lower bounce and have less forward momentum (although the skidding effect of the ball played with slice should be noticed).

Sidespin (Fig 40)

It is now possible to complicate the issue of topspin and slice by adding sidespin. Once again, if it is produced intentionally, particularly when slicing the ball, you add another dimension to the art of spinning the ball.

When played with sidespin and slice, the ball will move through the air sideways and forwards, and after bouncing it will continue in a sideways movement.

If you experiment with hitting the ball on different trajectories, increasing or decreasing the amount of spin, you will notice a different effect on a ball travelling through the air and after the bounce.

After a little practice, even by simply dropping a series of balls and hitting them

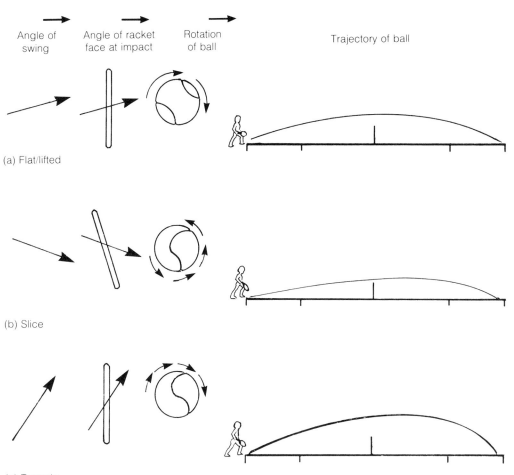

Angle of swing　　Angle of racket face at impact　　Rotation of ball　　Trajectory of ball

(a) Flat/lifted

(b) Slice

(c) Topspin

Comparisons between shots, based upon hitting at the same speed at varying heights over the net.

(a) Flat/lifted, hit about 3 feet over the net, will land very near the baseline.

(b) Slice, hit about 1 foot over the net, will land very near the baseline.

(c) Topspin, hit about 5 feet over the net, will land very near the baseline.

Conclusions

(b) For slice to go in court it must either be hit lower over the net or more slowly.

(c) Topspin can be hit harder over the net to reach a point near the baseline.

Fig 39　Types of spin.

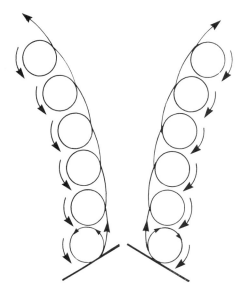

Fig 40 Left: backhand sidespin.
Right: forehand sidespin.

over the net with these suggested spins, you will realise how the *head* and the *face* of the racket must be in control to create these spins effectively. The fundamentals of stroke play, therefore, still apply.

These spins will also play an effective part when you are serving and when you are playing in the front of the court, volleying and smashing. We will look at the spin in these situations in the final part of the chapter.

FOREHAND DRIVE

Topspin *(Fig 41)*

Using the Eastern grip

Technical Points

1. Maintain firm grip on the racket.
2. Earlier preparation than normal is

required.
3. Normal backswing.
4. Before beginning the forward swing the racket head should be much lower than the striking height of the ball.
5. Use a hard brushing action up and forwards against the back of the ball.
6. Racket face is vertical to the ground at impact.
7. Controlled wrist action after the hit to encourage racket head speed.
8. Racket face closes during the follow-through.
9. Body weight follows through upwards and forwards.
10. Maintain balance throughout.

Tactical Value

1. Allows more margin for error when hitting aggressively or defensively from any part of the court.
2. Gives a higher trajectory over the net.
3. Higher bounce may cause problems for opponent.
4. Causes the ball to drop quickly to the feet of a volleyer.
5. Allows increased angles to be played.
6. Useful for counter-attack and change of pace (upsetting the opponent's rhythm).

Slice *(Fig 42)*

Using the Eastern grip

Technical Points

1. Basic forehand grip.
2. Normal backswing.
3. Before beginning the forward swing the racket head is well above the striking height of the ball.
4. Hit down and through the ball with the racket face slightly open.

(a)

(b)

(c)

(d)

(e)

(f)

Fig 41   Forehand drive with topspin.

(a)

(b)

(c)

(d)

(e)

(f)

Fig 42   Forehand drive with slice.

5. Make a firm impact under the back of the ball.
6. Keep the wrist firm and the weight of the body going into the shot.
7. Feel that you are holding the ball on the strings longer than in the basic drive.
8. On the follow-through the face of the racket remains open.
9. Body weight follows the direction of the ball.
10. Maintain balance throughout.

Tactical Value

1. It is good for defensive play when under pressure from the speed, height, width or length of the ball.
2. The lower bounce created by slicing the ball could give your opponent problems.
3. A useful tactic when approaching the net.
4. Helps accuracy of placement.
5. Allows better control in windy conditions and is particularly effective on slow damp courts and grass courts.
6. Useful for changing the pace and upsetting your opponent's rhythm.

BACKHAND DRIVE

Topspin (*Fig 43*)

Using the Eastern Grip

Technical Points

1. Basic backhand grip.
2. Earlier preparation than normal is required.
3. Normal backswing.
4. On the forward swing the racket head is much lower than the striking height of the

ball.
5. Use a hard brushing action up and forwards against the back of the ball.
6. Racket face is vertical to the ground at impact.
7. Controlled wrist action over the back of the ball to encourage overspin towards the chosen target area.
8. Racket face closes during follow-through.
9. Body weight follows through upwards and forwards.
10. Maintain balance throughout.

Tactical Value

1. Allows more margin for error when hitting aggressively or defensively from any part of the court.
2. Gives a higher trajectory over the net.
3. The higher bounce may cause problems for your opponent.
4. Causes the ball to dip quickly to the feet of a volleyer.
5. Allows increased angles to be placed.
6. Useful for counter-attack and change of pace (upsetting your opponent's rhythm).

Two-handed Topspin (*Figs 44 & 45*)

These points apply in exactly the same way to the two-handed player, who can certainly play incredible angles when using heavy topspin. When playing heavy topspin two-handed players drop the head of the racket much more than single-handed players, mainly because of the rolled wrist of the bottom hand.

(a)

(b)

(c)

(d)

(e)

(f)

Fig 43   Backhand drive with topspin.

(a)

(b)

(c)

(d)

(e)

(f)

Fig 44　Two-handed backhand drive with topspin.

Fig 45   Eduardo Velez of Mexico playing a two-handed backhand with
topspin.

Slice (*Fig 46*)

Using the Eastern Grip

Technical Points

1. Basic backhand grip.
2. Normal backswing.
3. On the forward swing, the racket head starts much higher than the striking height of the ball.
4. Hit down and through the ball with the racket face slightly open.
5. Make a firm impact under the back of the ball.
6. Keep the wrist firm and the weight of the body going into the shot.
7. Feel that you are holding the ball on the strings longer than for a basic drive.
8. Throughout the follow-through the racket face remains open.
9. Body weight follows direction of the ball.
10. Maintain balance throughout.

(a)   (b)   (c)

(d)   (e)   (f)

Fig 46 Backhand drive with slice.

Fig 47   Henri Leconte playing a
           backhand with slice.

Tactical Value

1. Good for defensive play when under pressure from the height, width or length of the ball.
2. The lower bounce may cause problems for your opponent.
3. A useful tactic for approaching the net.
4. Helps accuracy and placement.
5. Allows for better control in windy conditions and is particularly effective on slow and damp courts.
6. Lends itself to subtle use of angles.
7. Upsets your opponent's rhythm.

Two-handed Slice

Two-handed players using slice will follow exactly the same principles as the single-handed player.

However, those players who hold the racket with both hands throughout the stroke when slicing appear to play less fluently than those who release one hand after impact. In recent years many of the world's best two-handed players have been playing more and more single-handed backhands, particularly when defending from the back of the court, with the same assurance as the single-handed player. There is no doubt that if you are a two-handed player with a sound basic grip, a single-handed backhand slice is well worth cultivating. Like those world class players, you will be broadening your two-handed stroke play.

LOB

Topspin (*Fig 48*)

The Grip

For the forehand lob use the forehand (Eastern) grip; for the backhand lob use the backhand (full Eastern) grip.

Technical Points

1. Normal backswing.
2. Racket head well below the striking height of the ball on the forward swing (low to high).
3. Hard brushing action up the back of the ball.
4. Wrist action over the back of the ball to create heavy topspin.
5. Body weight goes upwards and forwards.
6. High follow-through.
7. Maintain balance throughout.

Fig 48   *Forehand lob with topspin*

Tactical Value

1.   Very aggressive lob against the volleyer, when there is plenty of time to set the shot up.
2.   Can quickly change a defensive situation into attack.
3.   Contains a strong element of surprise.
4.   Different trajectory of the ball can cause problems for the net player.
5.   Can force your opponent to keep further away from the net than normal.
6.   The fast bounce of the ball after landing makes any recovery shot extremely difficult.

Slice

The Grip

For the forehand lob use a forehand Eastern grip; for the backhand lob use a grip somewhere between a backhand Eastern and a chopper service grip.

Technical Points

1. Racket swings down and under the ball at impact (high to low).
2. Racket face well open.
3. Keep wrist firm.
4. Imagine holding the ball on the strings longer than for the basic lob.
5. Body weight goes upwards and slightly forwards.
6. Low follow-through.
7. Maintain balance throughout.

Tactical Value

1. Strong in defensive situations.
2. Holds the ball in the air, allowing you time to recover a good court position.
3. Different trajectory causes problems for the net player.
4. Helps accurate placement of the ball.

SERVICE SPINS

The early introduction of spin on the service is an aid to overall security. It helps to develop a sound, aggressive second service, and can help to eliminate many double faults. As the server's confidence grows in the security of spin on the second service, it will encourage him to become more aggressive on the first service – knowing that he is unlikely to serve a second service fault.

As we mentioned earlier, spin on the service is an important requirement for the high level player. Although the principles of spin are the same, hitting with spin from above your head will give you a completely different effect because the swing of the racket is now:

1. On a different plane from the ground-strokes.
2. Making contact with the ball in a different area.
3. Bringing in regular sidespin.

In your early practice you may not like the chopper grip, but work towards it gradually because to be a really good server you must finally arrive at this very flexible grip. The chopper grip is the key to developing the all-round spin effects of serving. To give you more options when serving on different courts and in different weather conditions, it is important that you develop a slice service and a topspin service.

Slice Service (*Fig 50*)

Using the chopper service grip

Technical Points

1. Placement of the ball is slightly further to the right of the body.
2. Racket face in a semi-closed position at impact.
3. Racket face continues its movement round the outside of the ball.
4. Maintain a strong throwing action.
5. Imagine holding the ball on the strings longer than for the basic service.
6. Body weight follows the direction of the ball.
7. Good follow-through.
8. Maintain good balance throughout.

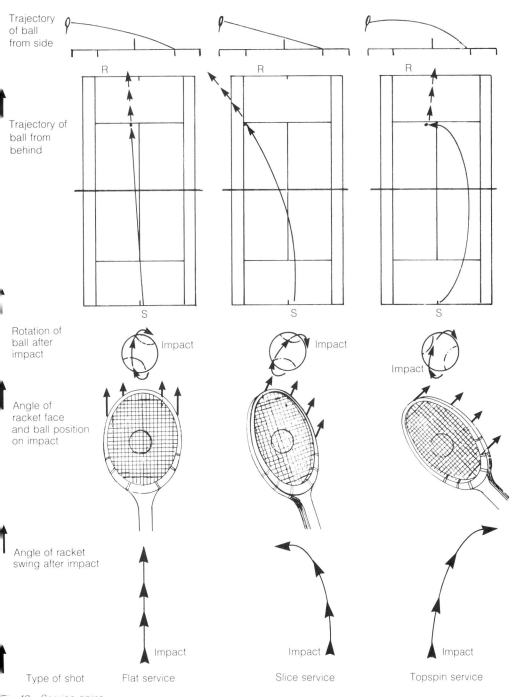

Trajectory of ball from side

Trajectory of ball from behind

Rotation of ball after impact

Angle of racket face and ball position on impact

Angle of racket swing after impact

Type of shot — Flat service — Slice service — Topspin service

Fig 49 Service spins.

(a)   *(b)*   *(c)*

(d)   *(e)*   *(f)*

Fig 50   Slice service.

Tactical Value

1. Takes opponent out of position because of the swing of the ball.

2. Forces your opponent to play shots too close to the body or too far away – upsets opponent's hitting area/contact point.

3. Useful variation to deceive opponent (different speed and flight of the ball).

4. Lower bounce may cause problems for opponent.

Topspin Service (*Fig 51*)

Using the chopper service grip

Technical Points

1. Placement of the ball on the left side of the body and slightly less forwards than for the basic service.
2. The back should be arched.
3. Upward brushing action of the racket face is essential.
4. Maintain strong throwing action.
5. Good wrist action to take the racket face up and across the ball.
6. Imagine the racket face turning over the top of the ball after impact.
7. Body weight follows the direction of ball upwards and forwards.
8. Maintain balance throughout.

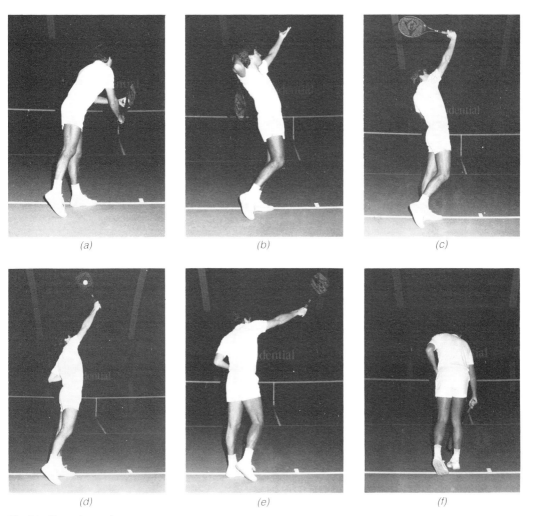

(a) (b) (c)

(d) (e) (f)

Fig 51 Topspin service.

Tactical Value

1. Allows for more margin of error (greater net clearance).
2. A higher, sharper bounce can cause problems for your opponent.
3. Aids aggression when used as a second service.
4. Higher trajectory of the ball over the net can give you more time to reach a good volleying position.

SUMMARY

Every ball you hit will have spin on it in one form or another. When you have the ability to control that spin and use it in a way that makes your opponent's hitting abilities less efficient, you have added a new dimension to your shot making.

Remember, you must have a good reason for putting spin on the ball, just putting spin on the ball for its own sake is not enough. Intentional spin broadens your tactical options and adds further quality to your game. It is a fascinating art.

Spin in all court areas will need regular practice which can be immensely stimulating and enjoyable while you are experimenting with all the different speeds, angles and degrees of spin. *Have fun with spin!*

4 Stroke Variations

Stroke variations are the extra strokes and methods that form part of the successful player's armoury. They do not fit into the basic strokes or the basic spins, although some of the variations will contain spin. They can generally be considered as specific shots for specific situations. This chapter will give the keen tennis player and the student of the game some worthwhile pointers as to how to play these variations well and, also, how to select the right time and place on the court in which to use them. Remember, it is no good just playing strokes for their own sake. They must always be played to attain a tactical objective and, ultimately, help you to win the points and the match.

RETURN OF SERVE
(*Fig 52*)

The return of serve is probably one of the most interesting and difficult situations in tennis. In half of the points in a game·it will be the first groundstroke you will play and yet it does not fit into normal groundstroke play because your opponent has far more possibilities than normal as with the ball in his hand he is under no pressure. Your return of serve has to be flexible enough to play solid attacking and solid defensive shots at a moment's notice.

The main objective is to put the ball into play regularly and, if possible, make it difficult for the server to play a successful second shot. As a receiver of service against a baseliner, you should generally aim to return the ball deep into the back of his court. As a receiver of service against a serve and volleyer, you should generally aim to return the ball to land near the service line.

In both instances, if the service is not very strong you should attempt to attack your opponent by the use of increased pace of shot or width of shot (aiming near sidelines) or a combination of both –

Fig 52   *Hana Mandlikova playing a strong backhand return of service.*

55

perhaps even turning the return of serve into an approach shot and following it to the net.

Use the grip for appropriate drives. Although sometimes there will not be time to change the grip if the service is fast, try to develop holding the racket firmly with a strong but flexible grip to enable you to deal with all levels of service.

Much of your success as a sound groundstroke player will depend on your ability to adjust your normal groundstroke play to the needs of returning the service. Bear the following points in mind:

1. The speed of the oncoming ball.
2. The swing and bounce of the ball created by spin.
3. Fast serves will mean hitting a rising ball.
4. There may be very little time to prepare.

To counter these points:

1. Be very alert and concentrate hard on watching the ball. The way your opponent uses the racket head and face may give you a clue to his intentions with each serve.
2. Trust the techniques of groundstroke play you have worked hard at perfecting.
3. Against a good first service use a *shortened backswing*. Continue the stroke with your sound techniques in these situations. Your returns will now be mainly instinctive.
4. Good, quick footwork is required to cope with a wide service.
5. Be ready to take advantage of a weaker service; this may be your opportunity to use your full swing.
6. Don't be tempted to hit too hard; use the speed of the oncoming ball, meeting it solidly with the weight of your body leaning

into the shot.
7. Check your position for returning serve in relation to the standard of serving. Don't position to favour your best shot; move *from* a good position to use your best shot. This way you give nothing away to your opponent.
8. *Above all else, get the ball over the net and in play.*

Technical Points

1. Alert position of readiness.
2. Balanced strong position, leaning forwards.
3. Flexible but strong grip.
4. Early movement diagonally forwards into the shot.
5. Racket backswing is dependent on the speed of the serve. When returning very fast serves shorten the backswing – almost play a volley action.
6. Hitting area/contact point should be well forwards. It will not always be possible to play at a comfortable distance or height.
7. Wrist firm at impact.
8. Weight going forwards into the shot.
9. Maintain balance throughout.
10. Quick recovery for the next shot.

Tactical Value

1. The ball should always be returned into play.
2. Where possible, play the ball into areas of the court that make it difficult for your opponent to be aggressive on his second shot.
3. Play to your opponent's known weaknesses.
4. Try to vary your returns of serve by: hitting to different areas; hitting at different speeds; hitting with different spins; varying your position on court for returning service.

To be effective on the return of serve, a player must be quick-thinking, adaptable, flexible and competent at constructing a dependable shot in far less time than normal. The return of serve is one of the most under-practised areas of tennis. If you want to be successful in match play do not just play matches – practise your return of serve on a regular basis. You will be very pleased at the beneficial results.

APPROACH SHOTS

The approach shot is extremely important to a player who, having developed a strong baseline game and sound net play, now needs to exploit these two skills. The baseline skills will force an opponent to play weak returns. With good approach shots a player can take advantage by moving towards the net, applying further pressure on the opponent by using strong net play.

Approach shots are usually thought of as being played against short balls (half court) when the player has to move forwards to play the ball. Because of this forwards movement and the position on court, it is easier to continue the movement towards a good volleying position than recover and return to the baseline. This short ball is a good starting point for developing an understanding of approach shots of *quality*. I emphasise quality because a poor approach will lose you the advantage gained and, probably, the point.

Approach shots can be played with all the groundstroke methods previously suggested and spin will also play an important part. The grips should be the normal grips used by the individual player when playing groundstrokes.

Technical Points

1. Alertness, often putting your opponent under pressure from previous groundstrokes (ready to move forwards).
2. Early preparation and movement in unison.
3. Even though you are on the move, get into a good hitting position (correct hitting area/contact point).
4. Maintain a sound technique throughout.
5. Firm hitting of the ball (basic topspin or slice).
6. Use smooth, rhythmical movements throughout, both in footwork and racket work.
7. Poise and balance are essential.

When playing approach shots with added sidespin:

8. Stance can remain more open (particularly on the forehand) – forwards movement will keep the weight into the shot.
9. Hitting area will be closer to the body when adding sidespin, creating a fading of the shot towards the sideline.
10. The racket face should be pulled inwards and forwards.

Tactical Value

1. Maintains advantage gained by previously played strong groundstrokes.
2. Maintains pressure already secured – do not let your opponent escape.
3. Forces your opponent into playing more difficult defensive strokes.
4. Stamps an authority over your opponent.
5. Leads to successful net play.

Fig 53   Jo Durie moving forward to approach the net.

quality give a player a ⸺ ⸺ ⸺ the baseline play and ⸺ play in the ⸺ of the court, taking the maximum advantage after forcing the opponent into weak, defensive situations. These mid-court approach shots are extremely important and need a lot of practice to groove the movement and technique for the quality of shot required. Do not let your opponent off the hook having established authority from the baseline.

Although the short ball is the obvious time to make your opponent move from the baseline to the front of the court, approach shots can be played from deeper or even shorter balls than suggested. When and how approach shots are played is in the hands of the player. An aggressive player may take more risks when playing approach shots; another will be more selective before approaching the net. Technical competence and self-confidence will play a large part in how you choose to move from the baseline to the front of the court. Try not to miss chances you have created. When you finally reach a good volleying position be prepared to use net play variations to maintain pressure on your opponent.

DROP SHOT (*Fig 54*)

This delicate shot is a 'must' in your all-round ability to play well tactically, particularly on a slow court where so much of the play is likely to be from the back of the court. Its greatest value is when playing against an opponent who prefers to control the play from the back of the court, giving you few opportunities to get into an attacking position. Played intelligently, the drop shot will give you the opportunity to move your opponent into the front of the court

and then take advantage of his position with a lob or passing shot. Because of its tactical value, players at all levels should try to develop an effective drop shot.

Use the grip for the appropriate drive.

Technical Points

1. Shape up for this stroke as if playing the drive.
2. Imagine stroking the face of the racket down the back and underneath the ball.
3. Take the speed off the ball.
4. Retain balance and feel on the ball.
5. The drop shot is a very personal stroke. It needs a delicate touch with backspin on the ball.
6. Needs extra care in watching the ball.
7. Needs eventually to be disguised, particularly when played from further back in the court.
8. Control of the racket face is extremely important.

Tactical Value

1. Useful against a slow mover.
2. Useful against a player who only likes to play from the baseline.
3. Can upset the rhythm of the ground-stroke player.
4. Can force a poor net player to the net.

VOLLEY VARIATIONS

Becoming a good, attacking net player is very demanding. It is not enough to be a good, basic volleyer dealing with balls above net height. You must be able to fight off the counter-attacking groundstrokes of an opponent. We have already looked at some of the basic volleys, now we shall look at some of the variations that are an

Fig 54   Catarina Lindqvist of Sweden playing a drop shot.

Low Volley (*Fig 55*)

Although this is only a change of hitting height for the volleyer, this shot poses many different problems. The players most likely to be in the low volley position are:

1. A player serving and then following his serve to the net.
2. A player who has been forced away from an attacking position at the net.
3. A player whose opponent can hit the

The low volley is generally considered to be a defensive stroke, although it is often played from an attacking position on court (the net). It is essential to play a careful well-placed shot to set yourself up for an easier next volley played from a higher, more aggressive position.

The grip is the same as for the basic volleys.

Fig 55 Ivan Lendl reaching for a low volley.

Technical Points

1. Short backswing.
2. Racket face open on impact to give lift.
3. Edge of racket close to the ground.
4. Very early impact.
5. Knees well bent, head over the ball.
6. Needs a firm but flexible wrist.
7. Played with control and feel, and often with backspin.
8. Move quickly to next position of readiness (generally closer to the net).

Tactical Value

1. Defensive position can be turned into an attacking position by precise placement.
2. Against a baseline player, place the volley near to the baseline.
3. Against a net player, place the volley on a short angle and keep the ball low over the net.
4. Do not try to hit fast winners from this position.
5. After playing a low volley regain a strong net position.
6. Well-played low volleys should enable a net player to regain the initiative.

Half Volley (*Fig 56*)

This ball is actually bouncing before the hit is made, and it is therefore, strictly, a groundstroke. The half volley can often be played from the back of the court closely following the technique of a forehand or backhand drive, but with a much fuller swing. However, because of its name, most players associate the half volley with the front of the court, and that is why we have included it in this section.

After you have played an approach shot, your opponent will certainly try to counter with either a low ball at your feet or a low ball played away from you. Well-played half volleys can maintain pressure on your opponent and enable you to attain a strong net position. Where possible, however, you should always try to play the low volley in preference to the more difficult half volley.

The grips for the half volley will be the normal grips used by the individual player when playing groundstrokes.

Technical Points

1. Short backswing.
2. Racket face square to the target, keep the wrist firm.
3. Edge of the racket head very close to the ground.
4. Point of impact well in front of the body.
5. Knees well bent and head down over the ball.
6. Stay well down during the follow-through.
7. Keep the stroke fluent.
8. Move quickly to next position of readiness (generally closer to the net).

Tactical Value

1. Maintains a good position on court when defending from the baseline.
2. Gives your opponent less time.
3. In mid-court, maintains the forwards movement to the net against low returns.
4. Helps recovery in difficult situations.

Stop Volley (*Fig 57*)

The stop volley is generally played by the net player when his opponent is defending outside his baseline and the net player is in a strong attacking position at the net. It is a very similar shot to the drop shot, although the ball is not bouncing, and most of the

Fig 56 Pat Cash playing a half volley.

Fig 57   John McEnroe playing a stop volley.

:echnical points are the same.

The grips will be the same as those used or basic volleys.

Technical Points

1. Short backswing, reduced follow-through.
2. Keep the wrist firm. Open the racket face at impact to increase backspin.
3. Watch the ball carefully.
4. Keep the head down over the ball.
5. Keep the knees bent.
6. Play the shot when the ball is net high or below.
7. Needs a very good touch.

Tactical Value

1. Keeps the ball very short in your opponent's half of the court.
2. Kills the speed of an attempted passing shot.
3. The element of surprise keeps your opponent back on his heels.
4. Useful against poor movers.

Drive Volley (Fig 58)

This volley is usually played from mid-court against a slow, shoulder high ball which requires attacking. The shot is generally more aggressive than a normal volley and is similar to a high forehand or backhand drive.

The grips will be the same as those used when playing groundstrokes.

Technical Points

1. Full backswing.
2. Swing forwards with the racket face closing over the ball at impact.
3. Play this shot when the ball is above

net height.
4. Continue your forwards momentum to the net.
5. Full follow-through.
6. Maintain controlled balance throughout.

Tactical Value

The drive volley allows outright attack against slow, high balls when close to the net or when coming to the net. To add a surprise element move off the baseline

Fig 58   Henrik Sundstrom of Sweden playing a drive volley.

quickly, not allowing a high, floating return to bounce.

Lob Volley *(Fig 59)*

The lob volley is generally played when players are facing each other in the net positions. It is a similar shot to the forehand and backhand lobs, but is played without backswing from a volley position.

The grips will be the same as those used when playing groundstrokes.

Fig 59   Hana Mandlikova playing a lob volley.

Technical Points

1. Short backswing.
2. Keep the wrist firm.
3. Open racket face at impact to give lift
4. Hitting area well in front of body.
5. Slight backspin.
6. Keep knees bent.
7. Short follow-through.
8. Needs a fine touch.

Tactical Value

1. Surprise.
2. Opponent loses his position close to the net.
3. Can make opponent stay further back than normal from the net.
4. Breaks opponent's volleying plans.

SMASH VARIATIONS

The smash, like many of the other strokes, has variations which are important in maintaining a high level of aggressive net play. The first of these is the jump smash, which is essential against very good deep lobs. The second is the slice smash, which is useful for deception and angling your smash. The third is the topspin smash which can be used against the most difficult deep lobs, those aimed deep over your backhand side. Finally, the backhand smash is used as a last resort if you are not able to play the stronger forehand smash.

Jump Smash *(Fig 60)*

Technical Points

1. Basic chopper grip.
2. Side-step back underneath the ball.
3. Long final step to impart the necessary

spring.
4. Quick side-stepping movement.
5. Quick recovery to next ready position.
6. Try to retain controlled balance throughout.

Tactical Value

1. Maintains attacking position against a good deep lob.
2. Enables a smash to be played rather than a defensive recovery shot.
3. Aids control of shot.

Fig 60   Boris Becker playing a difficult jump smash.

Slice Smash

Technical Points

1. Basic chopper grip.
2. Keep the ball on the right-hand side of the body as for the slice service.
3. Close the racket face slightly at impact.
4. Good follow-through.

Tactical Value

1. Angles the ball away from your opponent.
2. Gives extra security when smashing lobs from the right-hand side of the court.
3. When hitting a short angle, it is useful to deceive your opponent.

Topspin Smash

Technical Points

1. Basic chopper grip.
2. Throw the racket face up and over the ball (as for topspin serve).
3. Arch the back.
4. Quick recovery to next ready position.
5. Maintain balance throughout.

Tactical Value

1. Used when the lob is over your backhand side.
2. Helps to maintain attacking position.
3. May give you more time to recover.

Backhand Smash (Fig 61)

Nothing is more exciting than watching a top class player refusing to concede a net position once it has been established. To be able to do this, the player must have no apparent weaknesses on either side. Most

Fig 61 *Pat Cash fully in control of a backhand smash.*

drives, possibly refining it by using a service chopper grip.

Technical Points

1. Side-step back underneath the ball.
2. Strong shoulder turn.
3. Racket face meets the ball squarely and slightly in front of the body.
4. Reach high.
5. Sharp wrist action to bring the racket head over the ball.
6. Recover quickly to a ready position.
7. Maintain balance throughout.

Tactical Value

1. Helps to retain attacking position at net.
2. Last resort against low, attacking lob over the backhand side.
3. Successful use of this shot makes for more evenly balanced positioning and net play.

SUMMARY

If you can volley securely and play the necessary overhead shots, you will have a chance of emulating the top players. This, however, will depend on your ability to overcome some of the problems encountered in regularly putting the ball into play from all areas of the court. Remember, the successful player should enjoy the challenge of acquiring new skills and developing an all-round capability. With practice you could turn your dream into reality.

defenders will try to lob over the player's weaker side (generally the backhand). The players will usually try to run round the backhand smash to play their stronger and more favoured forehand smash. This, however, is not always possible and it will be necessary from time to time to play the more difficult backhand smash.

The grip is the same as for the backhand

5 The Improving Game

People often comment that although they know *how* they want to play their shots when it comes to playing the ball it is never as easy as it seems. It is always difficult to see our own mistakes and, more importantly, to overcome them. This section is intended to help you to overcome some of the more common problems.

If you have a specific recurring problem you may be able to diagnose the possible cause for the problem and take the correct action using the chart. If your problem or solution does not appear here don't despair; try to use your existing knowledge to diagnose the possible cause and effect yourself.

DIAGNOSIS CHECKLIST

First of all, choose the particular shot you wish to improve. Try to choose the area of the fundamentals that gives you the most cause for concern. If your answer to a question is yes, move down the column to the next question. If your answer to a question is no, ask yourself why not. This answer could point to another fundamental further up the column and thus point you to your area of improvement. The chart should be used not only for eradicating weaknesses but also for improving strengths.

Remember, the fundamentals are all interlinked and when they are used efficiently they will help to form a sound stroke which is the basic requirement for every player. When a player adds strategy to the sound strokes he is well on the way to developing the art of being not only a good stroker of the ball but a sound match player.

Watching the Ball

1. Are you reacting early?
2. Are you anticipating your probable 'hitting area' on the court?
3. Are you noticing any spin on the ball?
4. Are you in the intended hitting area?
5. Have you met your intended contact point?

Footwork

1. Are you in a good ready position?
2. Are you quick off the mark?
3. Are you arriving in good time?
4. Are you setting up a good hitting position prior to impact?
5. Are you recovering quickly after your shot?

Balance

1. Are you balanced in the ready position?
2. Are you balanced at the end of your run to the ball?
3. Are you balanced prior to impact?
4. Are you balanced on contact?
5. Are you balanced after impact?

Control of the Racket Swing

1. Are you preparing early on the backswing?

Fig 62 Boris Becker with his former coach Gunther Bosh. A coach is
important for improvement at all levels.

2. Do you have a mental picture of your
intended shot?
3. Is your backswing smooth and efficient?
4. Are you swinging forwards in good
time?
5. Are you using the forwards swing you
intended (shape of the shot)?

Control of the Racket Face

1. Are you using the correct grip?
2. Is the racket face under control on the
backswing?
3. Are you hitting the ball at the correct
contact point?
4. Is your wrist firm at contact?
5. Is the racket face pointing towards the
target?

PROBLEMS AND SOLUTIONS

If you genuinely want to improve your
game, be honest with your assessment of
the problem areas and try to diagnose the
specific points. Always remember too that
tennis skills do not remain constant without
thought and practice.

Service Basics

Service

Problems	Possible Reason	Possible Correction
Failing to hit at maximum height even when the ball is placed in the air correctly.	Letting the ball drop too far before the hit.	Hit the ball while it is 'stationary' in the air.
Loss of balance just before impact, even though the ball placement is correct.	1. Drawing the rear foot up to the leading foot, losing stability for the strong throwing action.	1. Do not let the rear foot move until after the ball has been struck.
Inability to serve with power or speed.	1. Pushing' the racket at the ball. No throwing action.	1. Practise 'throwing' action without the racket using tennis ball. Progress to racket throwing action. Develop racket head speed.
	2. Poor ball placement in wrong hitting area.	2. Practise ball placement without hitting the ball.
Inability to place the ball in the air correctly.	1. Flicking wrist.	1. Try to place ball in air with locked wrist.
	2. Letting ball go too soon.	2. Hold on to ball until it reaches shoulder height.
	3. Jerky action; bending elbow.	3. Keep a smooth rhythm and firm elbow.

Groundstroke Basics

Groundstrokes

Problems	Possible Reason	Possible Correction
Inability to repeat the intended stroke. No real method.	Loss of good positioning; breakdown of fundamentals; poor hitting area.	Practise against easy balls perfecting basic stroke. Concentrate on achieving the correct hitting area/contact point.
Balls continually going out to the right.	Hitting the ball too late, very close to the body, pushing the racket away from the body. Failure to control the racket head.	Practise hitting cross-court; check hitting area; hit in front; make the racket head swing in direction of target. Get the racket back early.
Balls being hit too long out of the court behind the baseline.	Hitting much too hard or with wrong racket face angle. Lack of control of the swing. Lack of control of the racket face. Loss of balance backwards.	Practise playing easy balls lower into target area. Point racket face in direction of target. Practise transferring weight from right foot to left, with body weight towards target.
Hitting too many balls in the net.	Not leaving enough margin for error. Uncontrolled wrist action. Lack of racket face control.	Practise hitting balls higher over the net. Imagine the net is six feet high. Keep wrist locked, with racket face pointing upwards.

The three most common groundstroke errors from the average player are:

1. Poor preparation, generally not starting the backswing early enough.

2. Getting too close to the ball.
3. Using too much wrist on shots.

So, never forget to practise the basics suggested in the early chapters.

Lobs

Problem	Possible Reason	Possible Correction
Not enough height over opponent.	1. Swing too shallow.	1. Swing more from low to high.
	2. Lifting head.	2. Watch the ball, not the opponent.
	3. Shortening swing.	3. Long follow-through, well above head height.
	4. Racket face too closed.	4. Open racket face prior to impact.
Mishitting ball.	1. Not watching ball on to racket.	1. Watch the ball, not the opponent.
	2. Jerky swing.	2. Make a slow, full, smooth swing.
	3. Late hitting area.	3. Play the ball in the correct hitting area, further forwards than for basic groundstrokes.

Netplay Basics

Volleys

Problem	Possible Reason	Possible Correction
Continually volleying shoulder high balls out of court.	1. Getting the racket hand ahead of the racket face (punching with the hand).	1. Punch with the racket face.
	2. Racket face laying back.	2. Point racket face towards target area.
Too many low volleys into the net.	Bending from the waist to play these volleys; racket head drops; loss of control.	1. Bend the knees. 2. Get the racket hand lower. 3. Open racket face. 4. Play an earlier ball (hitting area).
Failure to get enough power.	1. Poor punching action.	1. Imagine punching a ball in front of you. Tighten grip on impact.
	2. Playing a late ball.	2. Check hitting area. Play ball in front of you. Reach forwards.
	3. Weak wrist on impact.	3. Keep firmer grip on the racket. Squeeze handle at impact.
	4. Falling back on impact.	4. Play earlier ball (contact point). Move forwards to meet the ball.

Smash

Problem	Possible Reason	Possible Correction
Hitting balls into the net.	1. Racket face pointing downwards.	1. Point racket face towards target area. Control wrist action.
	2. Ball too far forwards.	2. Move underneath the ball; check hitting area; remain sideways. Try to copy service throwing action.
Missing the ball.	1. Not watching the ball carefully.	1. Watch the ball all the time, not the target.
	2. Too much use of the body.	2. Try to copy service throwing action. Maintain balance at impact.
	3. Trying to hit too hard.	3. Hit at half speed; make good placement.

Service Spins

Topspin Service

Problem	Possible Reason	Possible Correction
Unable to produce topspin.	1. Not enough racket head movement up and across the ball.	1. Relax the wrist. Try to hit the ball from 'low to high'.
	2. Wrong angle of racket face at impact.	2. Imagine hitting the ball at bottom and left and brushing across to the top and right of the ball.
	3. Racket head speed too slow.	3. Accelerate racket head as you strike the ball.
Ball not bouncing forwards with topspin.	Not enough wrist action.	Exaggerate the use of wrist. Stronger brushing action. Try to hit from low to high on the ball. Maintain racket head speed throughout.

Service Slice

Problem	Possible Reason	Possible Correction
Unable to produce spin.	Angle of racket face at impact.	1. Hit specific part of the ball, i.e. right-hand side. 2. Imagine cutting a piece off the right-hand side of the ball.
Ball going too far to the left.	Racket face angle at impact.	1. Aim to the right of the target. 2. Wrong placement of the ball; usually too far left.

Groundstroke Spins

Topspin

Problem	Possible Reason	Possible Correction
Unable to produce topspin.	1. Wrong swinging action.	1. Exaggerate swinging from very low to very high to create a better upward swing.
	2. No brushing action on the ball.	2. Don't hit the ball forwards so hard. Try to make the ball revolve towards the target. Aim high over the net.
Topspin goes into the net.	1. Backswing preparation too high.	1. Have very low position of racket head at the beginning of the forwards swing.
	2. Angle of swing too flat.	2. Swing from very low to very high (brushing action).
	3. Closed racket face at impact.	3. Keep racket face vertical to the ground on impact.

Slice

Problem	Possible Reason	Possible Correction
Unable to produce slice.	1. Preparation too low.	1. At the beginning of the forwards swing the racket head should be at shoulder height.
	2. Racket face angle not correct.	2. Open racket face on contact with the ball. Imagine holding the ball on the strings longer than normal.
	3. Angle of swing too flat.	3. Swing from high to low (cutting the bottom of the ball).
Unable to hit to a length with slice.	Racket stops immediately after impact. Little follow-through.	Finish with racket follow-through continuing towards the target.

6 The Practising Game

PRACTISE FOR SUCCESS

Practice makes perfect, so the saying goes, and although it may not be completely true high level players are always striving for greater perfection of performance. They know that only practice will fulfil their particular dream.

Thoughtful practice at whatever level will push you that little bit nearer to playing more consistently and maximising your ability. *Confidence*, such an important factor in playing well, will be raised with the belief that you can produce sound stroke play and tactical moves at any given time. Practice can make all dreams a reality.

Regular controlled practice can:

1. Improve your technique.
2. Improve and groove your method.
3. Improve your consistency.
4. Improve your control and placement of the ball.
5. Improve your overall game.
6. Improve your understanding of the game.
7. Be very enjoyable.

Most good match players are also good practice players. They *enjoy* practice, keeping their strokes in order and constantly working at any flaws that need eradication. They enjoy expending the effort and energy that top level play demands, always aware that practice is vital if they are to reach their goals in the game. Watching them in play and practice, they give th impression of hitting balls with no appare effort and with what appear to be complete ly automatic movements and actions. The have probably forgotten about the man hours spent working on their game, repea ing again and again the basic strok requirements, the variations, the use c spin, and developing the tactical values c each aspect. Work and practise the certainly did, and it is equally certain tha they did it with a great deal of physical an mental effort.

Planning your Practice

Time

How much time should you spend ir practice? The answer depends on severa things, not the least of which will be your level of aspiration. How good do you *really* want to be? The answer to this question wil govern how much you will practise.

Plan your practice sessions into smal periods of time and don't worry if other players appear to be improving at a quicker rate than you are. No one can predict eventual levels of skill attainment. Your rates of learning will always vary. Don't be disheartened; keep to a sensible timed programme and you *will* improve.

Structure

To get the most out of your practice time, work on some specific points of stroke play, shots and tactics. For this, consider the ree different roles you will have to play at ny given time in a match:

. Your role when defending.
. Your role when attacking.
. Your role when counter-attacking.

ou must also consider two other factors:

. Your own planning and shot selection when you are able to dictate the play.
. Your ability and sound stroke play when your opponent is dictating the play.

Having considered these three different roles and who is dictating the play, you may well come to the conclusion, for example, that you are at your best when attacking but are less secure when defending. Why, is the next question you must answer. Whatever your answer is you are now *thinking correctly*, and by treating other aspects of your play in exactly the same way you can plan your practice programme.

Practise to Win

t is vital in all forms of practice that the work you do relates to match play situations. t is of little value developing into a technically skilled player and yet in matches choosing the wrong shot options and missing opportunities. This happens so often: the opening shots in the point have been played well, forcing the opponent into a weak reply, but then the player fails to make a good choice of shot to win the point.

Improving the area of shot selection can be achieved by practising simple tactical situations, repeating the same moves over and over again. As you become more confident your practice partner should gradually increase the pressure on you.

This can be done in a variety of ways – by adding speed, applying more spin, hitting balls wider – whilst you try to maintain the level of performance achieved before the pressure increased.

One strong piece of advice: never be reluctant to return to a simpler practice if too many errors begin to creep in when working under pressure. Take time out to discover why the error is occurring.

Disciplining your thinking and approach in practice is a sure way of becoming a player who uses stroke play intelligently and not one who just hits tennis balls with technical skill. Remember, you are trying through practice to become a *better tennis player*. It is important, therefore, to plan your practice sessions around the reality of match play. Your ultimate aim should be performance under pressure.

PRACTICE METHODS

Many of you will know the story of Borg's early days, hitting ball after ball against the doors of his father's garage. I am sure he established his method of play in that environment, repeating over and over again his now famous technique. Within the confines of such a small area his footwork and reactions would also have had to be very good to rally so consistently. The following are methods you can use to practise.

Wall Practice

Wall practice is probably the oldest method of individual practice. Using the wall intelligently can do much to improve your technical quality and footwork. Controlled rallying of your groundstrokes will give you the repetitive practice to consolidate your

Fig 63 Stefan Edberg with his coach Tony Pickard. Top international players must practise regularly.

basic technique. Work at applying spin to these techniques, building up the confidence that comes with sound stroke play.

The wall is quite an opponent: it returns your serve, outplays you with groundstrokes, and can outvolley you. What better opponent could you choose to help you, continually returning balls for you to practise?

Ball Machine

The ball machine can be controlled in such a way as to give players of differing standards the opportunity to practise. With varying speed, flight of ball, direction and even spin, this machine can help to build up your skills. Constant repetition of these variations is very important for your understanding of how the ball can travel towards you, and how to respond and play against each. It is usually used on a tennis court, and the results of your returns can be assessed.

Partners

Practising with a co-operating partner brings you the reality of the tennis court and an 'opponent'. Your partner will not be quite as accurate at placing the ball as the wall or the ball machine, but it is the uncertainty of his play that will strengthen your powers of concentration, alertness and movement about the court. The playing of good shots will be rewarded, and in practice sessions this is good for morale and confidence.

The choice of partner is important, he must be willing to go along with you in genuine thoughtful practice. One of the major misconceptions about choosing a practice partner is that he should have a higher standard of play. This may be true for the player who is secure technically and may need to play sets and matches to take his game to a higher standard, but for the less able player a partner who is willing simply to feed balls repetitively can give you valuable help.

The following are examples of fairly common co-operating practice partners:

1. A coach who may no longer be as good a player as one of his pupils is able from knowledge and experience to create situations, feeding single balls or by rallying, for his pupil to practise any part of the game successfully.
2. A parent whose child needs to practise before his next tennis session should be capable of helping him to improve by using simple feeding methods. The parent should use a basket of balls and hit single balls like a ball machine.

Anyone who is willing to hit (or even throw) tennis balls to you in a controlled manner will be of value to your practice sessions.

Tennis is generally considered to be an individual game. However, in order to improve it is beneficial for two individuals to form a 'team'. Don't be selfish — work together as a team and you will both benefit from this co-operation.

PRACTICES AND DRILLS

The following practices should give you a pointer as to what may be possible with your playing partner, whatever your standard. Use your imagination to create other tennis situations you may wish to practise.

Groundstroke Practices

Practice One (Fig 64)

First play simple rallies with your partner, using the opposing two squares. Use gentle forehand and backhand drives. Make sure that you use the racket head and racket face correctly. Keep the feet moving with good positioning.

Continue the same practice but take a new position half-way between service line and baseline. Use good footwork and racket work.

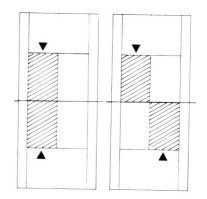

Fig 64

Practice Two (Fig 65)

Now use the full length of the court, continuing the simple rallying with gentle forehands and backhands. Increase movement by returning to the centre of the court after every shot. Increase the tempo of your rallies and bring variations into play (straight and cross-courts). Play for points.

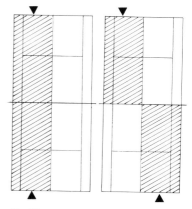

Fig 65

Practice Three (Fig 66)

Playing back to the same target area will extend your movement about your own half of the court. Try to maintain a sound technique under pressure using basic and variation stroke play. At the same time try to improve your accuracy. Aim to a given point controlled by your partner who should vary his shots to any part of the court beyond the service line. Should his shots fall in the service squares, you should play approach shots and eventually move to the net and use your volleys and smashes. This should form a strong part of your practice when developing your attacking play. Pressure can be increased by your partner hitting balls in different areas of your half of the court from his volleying position.

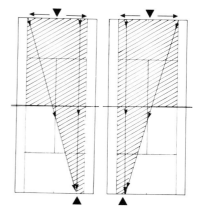

Fig 66

Net Play Practices

Using the same court areas as for the groundstrokes you can now go through your net play programme.

1. Gentle close volleying; move back to the limit of the shaded area to practise low volleys and half volleys.
2. Do the same routine cross-court.
3. From the full extent of his court, your partner plays groundstrokes. You continue to volley. Practise a variety of volleys. Your partner can change the practice to develop your smash. Later, mix groundstrokes and lobs into the exercise for fast reaction and footwork.
4. Do the same routine cross-court.
5. With your partner in the 'fixed' area of the court, you can practise your groundstrokes, selecting the right ball to approach the net and developing approach shots. Now volley and smash, aiming all your shots into the fixed area of the court.

Progress to using the entire court area for groundstroke and net play practice. Use a scoring method for developing competition between you and your partner. The only co-operation you require in this competitive exercise is that both players try their hardest to win all the points.

Service Practice

Service practice is easily achieved by taking on court a basket of balls and serving into the service squares and then into selected areas of the squares. You should learn to serve accurately, using your basic service and its variations, trying to develop sound technique in all methods.

You may still need a co-operating partner to help you check the technical points.

While you have a rest, you, in turn, can check out your partner's technical points.

Don't forget, you can also practise your service against a wall.

From this point, all your groundstroke practices should begin with a service, both in a straight line and cross-court. If you are practising service plus groundstrokes and net play you should do this for a set amount of time. Your partner should then serve for the same period. This will allow you to practise your return of service whilst he practises his service.

All the practices suggested should have you working technically and tactically, practising defence, counter-attack and attack. By repeating these over and over again you should be able to raise your standard of play.

Fig 67 Martina Navratilova and Pam Shriver sharing a word on tactics in a doubles game.

83

The Practising Game

Match Play Practice

You should follow most practice sessions by playing sets. This is the time to test your work on the practice court by playing matches. You will be able to see the rewards of planning your practice and spending time practising those situations that are needed in matches.

A Selection of Drills

Groundstroke Consistency (*Fig 68*)

Purpose To develop control and consistency.

Description The players rally the ball counting the number of successful hits.

Variations As control develops, the players:

1. Stand further back.
2. Play faster shots.
3. Play a variety of shots.
4. Aim at targets.

Target Serving (*Fig 69*)

Purpose To improve accuracy of serve.

Description Aim at various targets in the service box. Count successful hits in service squares and at target (three feet square).

Variations

1. Try spin serves.
2. Use a scoring system up to 11 points: 1 for a service square, 5 for a target, minus 1 for a fault.

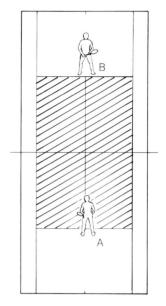

Fig 68

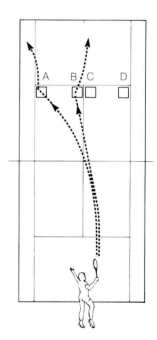

Fig 69

Basic Drive Practice (Fig 70)

Purpose To develop consistency and accuracy on the swing.

Description Feeder sends easy balls one at a time from baskets. Player aims to develop a grooved and rhythmic swing by repeating the same shot. Count successful shots.

Variations

1. Choose smaller target areas.
2. Hit the ball harder.
3. Play from other areas of the court.

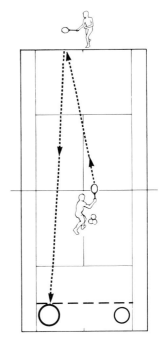

Fig 70

Linking Forehand and Backhand Drives (Fig 71)

Purposes To develop movement and to encourage changing grips.

Description Feeder sends easy balls alternately to forehand and backhand side. Count successful shots.

Variations

1. Choose smaller target areas.
2. Feeder varies his pattern.
3. Player varies his target areas.

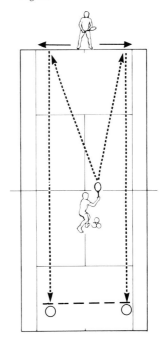

Fig 71

The Practising Game

Anchor Running (Fig 72)

Purpose To develop player's control under pressure of movement and his ability to recover to a ready position.

Description Feeder on baseline sends single balls to player's forehand corner. After every shot player has to recover to the ready position in the centre of the court. Count successful shots.

Variations

1. Give player less time between shots.
2. Choose other target areas.
3. Play from other areas of the court.

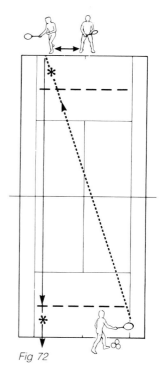

Fig 72

Running Drives (Fig 73)

Purpose To develop accurate hitting under pressure of movement and to rally consistently.

Description One player hits straight drives. The other player hits cross-court drives. Each player will play alternate shots, forehand and backhand etc., and from alternate sides of the court.

Variations

1. Players reverse roles.
2. Count the number of shots in a rally.
3. Play competitively. First player to score 11 points is the winner.

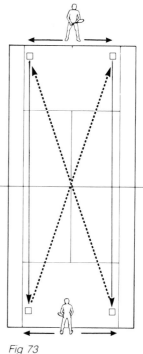

Fig 73

Groundstroke/Volley Rally (Fig 74)

Purposes

1. To improve accuracy on drives and volley.
2. To develop consistency in rallying.
3. To practise singles play with four players on court.

Description Four players share the court, using half the court lengthwise for each pair. In a pair, one player is a volleyer and the other a groundstroke player and they keep a rally going independently of the other pair. Count successful shots. Note: two balls are being used on one court so be aware of the safety factor.

Variations

1. Change sides.
2. Players play cross-court.
3. Players play competitively.
4. Pairs compete against each other.

Close Volley Consistency (Fig 75)

Purposes To develop control and consistency and to quicken anticipation and reflexes.

Description Two players rally the ball counting the number of successful hits.

Variations As control develops:

1. Vary positions on court.
2. Play faster shots.
3. Play a variety of shots.
4. Play competitively.

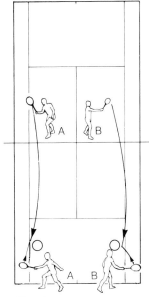

Fig 74

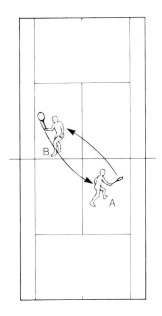

Fig 75

The Practising Game

Scramble Volley (Fig 76)

Purposes

1. To develop quick reactions.
2. To play a variety of shots.
3. To develop movement.

Description Feeder sends balls to either side of player to simulate a rally. Feeder hits single balls, but does not rally. Player must try to return every ball into play. Count successful shots.

Variations

1. Player plays from mid-court (no man's land).
2. Feeder occasionally lobs.
3. Player must aim at specified target area on all shots.

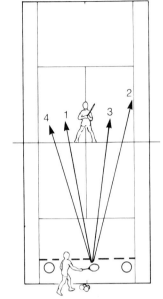

Fig 76

Serve/Volley (Fig 77)

Purposes

1. To develop aggressive serving.
2. To develop following service to the net.
3. To practise and develop first volley mid-court.
4. To develop controlled movement.

Description Player serves into service square and follows service to the net (a). Feeder does not return the service but hits the ball from his hand at service line (b). Player plays first volley and continues to the net. Feeder does not play the ball but hits it from his hands for volleyer. Note: the correct timing of the feeding is important.

Variations

1. Aim at specific targets.

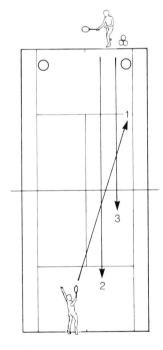

Fig 77

2. Feeder adds a lob on fourth shot.
3. Feeder increases the difficulty.

Four Ball Sequence Groundstrokes, Approach and Volley (Fig 78)

Purposes

1. To link various shots together.
2. To develop tactical ability.
3. To develop movement to the net.

Description   Feeder sends balls one at a time from the basket:

1. Deep to forehand.
2. Deep to backhand.
3. Short to forehand approach.
4. Short to forehand volley.

Player aims at targets in back corners.

Variations

1. Vary feeding pattern.
2. Vary target pattern.
3. Increase speed of feed.

Volley and Smash (Fig 79)

Purposes

1. To develop reflexes.
2. To develop recovery to the net.
3. To practise the smash realistically.

Description   Feeder rallies with partner sending first a low volley, then a smash and so on. Feeder can use single ball feeding if the rally keeps breaking down. On all shots the player must try to play the ball before it bounces.

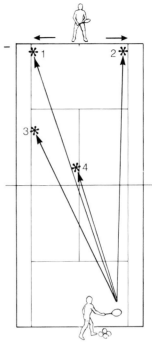

Fig 78

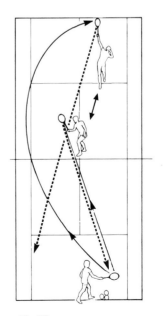

Fig 79

Variations

1. Increase tempo.
2. Vary pattern of feeds.

PRACTICE CHECKLIST

1. For practice sessions decide what shot sequence or situation you are going to practise.
2. Start with gentle shots which help to develop rhythm and control and try to groove the shot before you increase the difficulty of the task.
3. Set attainable targets, for example count the number of shots over the net and into the court.
4. Pick target areas in the court.
5. Aim at targets placed on the court.
6. Bring in a variety of shots.
7. Try to vary the length and direction of your shots.
8. Try to link together shots as in a match, for example groundstroke – approach shot – volley. Create a realistic situation.
9. Play a role. For example, if you are a groundstroke player who doesn't like to play at the net, imagine you are a net rusher and go to the net at every opportunity in your practice session.
10. Play controlled games of 11 points. A controlled game means that one player plays aggressively and the other plays a defensive game (swop roles).
11. Play a match and evaluate your partner's performance. This is good for tactical analysis. Discuss each other's performance afterwards.
12. Co-operate with your practice partner to achieve beneficial results.

SUMMARY

Learning to play well takes time – time spent on the practice court playing matches, analysing your play, returning to the practice court, working hard on all the points learned from them, repeating the whole performance over and over again. If you can learn how to practise you will almost certainly have learned how to improve.

We hope this chapter will have prodded you into going to the tennis court to practise, armed with many new thoughts and ideas. We hope also that you will find that well-constructed practice sessions can be fun, stimulating and rewarding. Keep your head down and your imagination flowing and you will find that the old saying of 'Practice makes perfect' still has a sound ring of truth.

Good luck and enjoy the competition; you will have earned it.

7 The Tactical Game

INTRODUCTION

We introduce this most important chapter with a quotation from a similar chapter written sixty years ago:

When the player has mastered the fundamental principles to the point of being able to put them into practice with certainty, he may allow himself to concentrate on tactics. It is no use going on to the court to play a singles match with a mind that is blank except for the idea of returning the ball over the net correctly. A plan of campaign is essential. Your opponent is going to make it as difficult as possible for you to observe those basic principles, and you for your part must have a plan which will secure you enough freedom to use the methods of play most suitable to you and which at the same time give your opponent less opportunities to use their favourite moves.

Many things have changed in sixty years, but thoughts on strategy and tactics have not.

Before you can implement strategy, you must have developed these skills:

1. The art of evaluating your own performance.
2. Understanding your own game.
3. Reading your opponent's game.

A quality player should be capable of regularly playing his own favourite game. This game must be based on sound principles and should become his normal method of play. He must, however, be able to adapt this method to suit the varying needs of match play. Take the example of a serve and volleyer on his favourite grass court surface. If he plays a singles match on a slow, high bouncing surface he will find it much more difficult to sustain his serve and volley game successfully against a player of his own standard. He must therefore adapt his game to the demands of the slow court surface. He will need the tactical awareness to appreciate the problem, but with technical and tactical soundness he should be able to construct an alternative to his normal strategy.

Tactical Awareness

You must be aware of what you are capable of achieving personally in the form of tactics and should not rush into trying new tactics in a match without having previously tested them in practice. However, if during match play it becomes obvious to you that your opponent is countering your favourite form of play rather well, you must make some changes. But how?

1. Look for weaknesses in your opponent's play while continuing to try and win points.
2. Assess your opponent's match plan and strategy, looking for any weakness.
3. Implement a new tactical plan.

If, for example, your favourite forehand down the line is less effective because your opponent is left-handed with a strong fore-

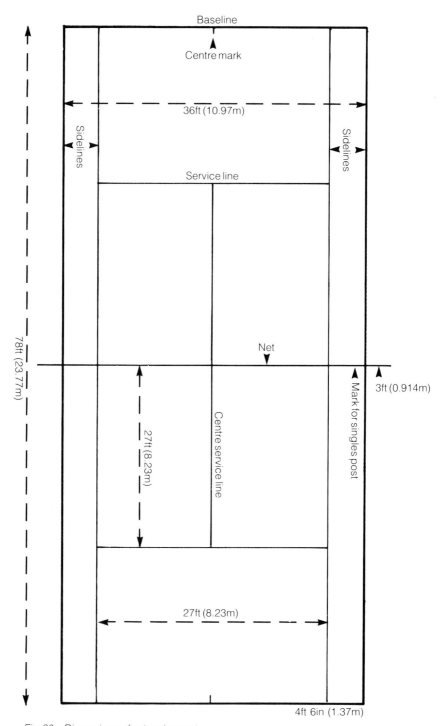

Fig 80   Dimensions of a tennis court.

and, you must be aware of the problem and adopt a strategy that can successfully overcome it.

The continual evaluation of your own performance and that of your opponent during a match is very difficult, but, if used successfully, can reap rewards.

BASIC MATCH PLAY TACTICS

These basic tactics are the foundation for all levels of play, but sometimes appear to be different when the top level players operate them. The reason for this is their more sophisticated stroke play and greater variety of strokes. When watching great players we tend to become excited with their stroke play and fail to watch their tactics and strategy. These are always founded on a basic formula and can be clearly followed if you can take your eyes off those great strokes and the excitement of the game.

The Singles Game

Basic Court Positions

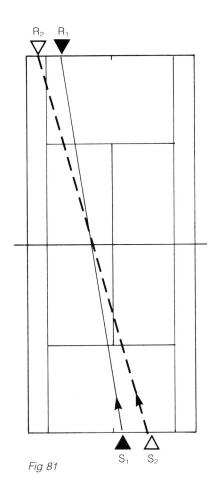
Fig 81

Service and return (Fig 81) Server is positioned behind the baseline near the centre mark (S_1), while the receiver is positioned just outside the baseline, covering both sides of the service square equally (R_1).

The server may adjust his position to create greater angles against the receiver (S_2), and the receiver may adjust his position to counteract any change of position by the server (R_2).

Rallying positions (Fig 82) The server and receiver are positioned 3 to 4 feet behind the baseline near the centre mark (S_1 and R_1). Players will adjust their positions to take account of varying angles and depths of shot. Players may decide to take up positions about 7 to 8 feet from the net (S_2 and R_2), where they will still adjust their positions to take account of varying angles, depths and heights of shot.

The positions on court are never fixed, they must reflect the pattern of play.

The Tactical Game

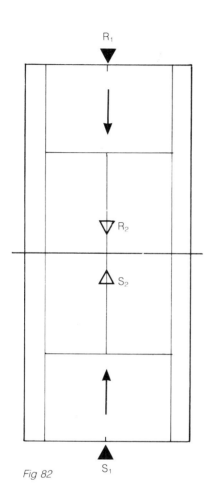

Fig 82

Basic Tactics

1. Retain good positions on court. The better your position on court related to the play, the easier it is to execute the stroke.
2. Put and keep the ball in play. Play the ball accurately to achieve your tactical objectives.
3. Make your opponent run. This strains his ball sense, judgement and timing.
4. Exploit any weaknesses.
5. Wrong-foot your opponent. This is the beginning of the art of not playing the obvious.
6. Be aware of the percentage game.
7. Be aware of your own strengths and weaknesses. The sounder your technical ability, the more chance you have of following your tactical plan.
8. Be patient.
9. Develop a game plan.

Good positioning Most players appreciate the need to move quickly to retrieve an opponent's shots, but fail to use the same quick movements to recover to a good ready position in relation to the play. Learn to respond to a good position from your own good shots: you will miss any opportunities of tactical superiority if you don't Always remember the basic court positions.

Put and keep the ball in play Try to hit the ball to a consistent length. If you can, keep your opponent behind the baseline where he will find it very difficult to hit a winning shot.

You don't have to hit 'winners' to win matches. Most matches are lost by a player making too many mistakes. If you *always* return the ball into play you will force your opponent into losing the match. The good player develops a balance between consistency and aggression.

Make your opponent run It is important to make sure that an opponent has little time in which to play his shots and that he has to keep changing his position to play the ball. It is easy to groove a shot by hitting it regularly from the same position, so if you don't want your opponent to get into a rhythm you must move him around the court in all directions and in a pattern which, hopefully, he cannot anticipate.

Fig 83 Pernfors and Lendl in a tough singles match on centre court.

The Tactical Game

Exploit a weakness Right from the open-ing practice shots in a match you should be assessing your opponent's play and searching for any weaknesses. Having discovered a weakness, remember it and work out a way of using it to your advantage.

There is a danger that playing to the weakness too often will alert your oppo-nent, who will then start positioning differ-ently for this continuous attack and escape the trap you have set. Don't overplay your hand, keep him guessing.

Wrong-foot your opponent This is prob-ably one of the most satisfying tactical moves. It is a direct follow-up of making your opponent run from side to side. Con-tinuing this theme of play, your opponent will begin to anticipate the next ball and possibly move too soon, allowing you to play the ball in the opposite direction.

A word of warning: it is nearly always the good quick movers you catch with this tactic. The slower moving player is still in the same area of the court when you decide to use the move and so will be waiting for it.

The percentage game You should always have a good understanding of your own capabilities in keeping the ball in play (consistency) and hitting an attacking shot (aggression). You should be able to evalu-ate your chance of success when playing a particular shot from previous experience in practice and matches. Based upon that information, you should choose a shot with a high percentage of success that will be suitable for your current situation.

There are four golden rules of percent-age match play:

1. Always try to put your first service into play.

2. Always put your return of serve int play.
3. Always put your first volley into play.
4. If in doubt, play your most reliable sho

Remember, if you hit the ball into the net c out of court, you will have no percentag chance of winning the point. So play to you strong and reliable shots and increase you chance of success.

The Doubles Game

Many players find the doubles game much more attractive to play; they feel more relaxed, enjoying the sensation of sharec responsibility. Indeed, there usually seem: to be more enjoyment and fun when play ing doubles.

Playing a good doubles game still relate: to good tactics and strategy, but now you are part of a team and must be aware of the strengths and weaknesses of both you partner and the opposition team. With thi information you should be able to plan a successful strategy for your team.

Basic Court Positions

Starting positions (Fig 84) Server is pos-itioned behind the baseline a little wider o the centre mark than for singles. Server's partner (SP) is positioned close to the net about half-way between the outside side-line and the centre service line. Receiver is in the same position as in singles. The receiver's partner (RP) is positioned just inside the left-hand service box at an equa distance between the inside sideline and the centre service line.

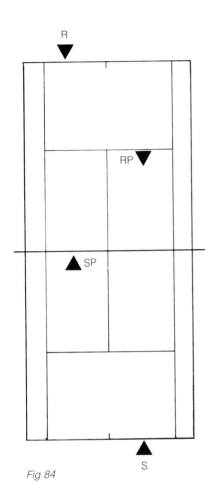

Fig 84

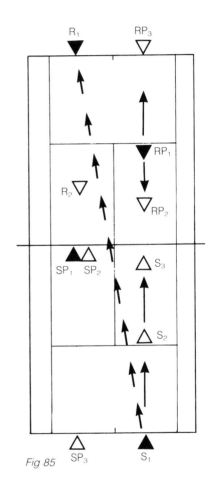

Fig 85

receiver.

Receiver may follow his return to the net (R_2) and join his partner (RP_2) in a balanced attacking position. Server's partner (SP_3), if lobbed, may join partner (S_1) on baseline and develop joint defensive position.

Playing positions (Fig 85) Players will change their positions to develop possible winning positions. Server may move from the baseline to mid-court (S_2) and then to the volley positions (S_3), developing a joint attacking position with partner. The positions of the receiver and his partner will be controlled by the standard of the return of service. The receiver will hold his position after returning the serve, while his partner may move forwards slightly (RP_2) or may decide to move back to the baseline (RP_3) to develop a joint defensive position with

Basic Tactics

1. Retain good positions on court. The better your team's position on court related to the play, the easier it is to execute the strokes.

Fig 86   Mens doubles – attacking net play.

2.   You are playing a team game, so all your tactics should be based on this.

3.   Get nearer to the net more quickly than your opponents so that you can hit the ball downwards while they are forced to hit the ball up and over the net.

4.   Keep the ball low over the net. This is very important when returning service.

5.   The sounder your team's technical ability, the greater the chance of keeping the ball in play and following your tactical plan.

6.   Play the ball accurately to open up the court, giving your partner the chance to win the point.

7.   Attack the weaker opponent.

8.   Win your service game.

9.   Be aware of the percentage game.

10.   Develop a game plan.

Remember, doubles is a team game: do you and your partner play well together? Are your strokes compatible?

SUMMARY

If you want to become a good match player in singles or doubles you need to develop an understanding of the court and the possible angles of play. You must play your own strengths while evaluating and exposing your opponent's weaknesses. You must be able to construct an effective game plan, while remaining flexible in your thinking in case you need to adjust or change it. You must believe in yourself and your ability to win based upon your sound strategy.

This may sound very complicated, but in reality it isn't. If you practise these aspects one at a time, you will simplify the skills of tactics and strategy.

Successful strategy will enhance your enjoyment of the game. Enjoy becoming a match winner!

8 The Physical Game

It is now becoming increasingly accepted by most tennis players that the physical demands of the game are such that players will not produce their best performance without first ensuring that they are in peak physical condition as a result of a regular and specific fitness training programme.

The rewards are plain to see – you are faster and more agile in reaching wide or short balls; you maintain your technique in the longer rallies because you do not get tired; you have more strength and power to hit harder volleys, serves and smashes for winners; and you have enough stamina to survive a long hard match. You will also be more mentally alert, you should avoid injury better and, above all, you will enjoy your game much more.

Work on your fitness training and become a tennis *athlete,* rather than an ordinary *player*!

FITNESS REQUIREMENTS

The unpredictability of tennis is that matches last as long as it takes to produce a winner. There is no time limit and a match can last for less than forty minutes or more than five hours. Just try to imagine the different mental and physical demands that would be required between playing for forty minutes on a fast court and winning (or losing) 6–0, 6–0, and slogging it out for hours in a long five-setter on a slow clay court. The only answer is to be fully prepared for the most difficult situation and

never go on court uncertain about your physical condition.

Look at the demands of a typical three set match with a result of 6–4, 5–7, 6–4. This would normally take about two hours to play under tournament conditions. The match contains 32 games and 200 points if an average of six points per game is assumed. Players have 1½ minutes to rest between every two games and are allowed a maximum of 30 seconds to prepare for each point. The *actual* playing time is therefore much reduced and probably amounts to only 40 to 50 minutes. If you consider that you have a short breather between each point and 1½ minutes of total rest every two games, you have to be either very unfit or play in an exceptionally long match before general fatigue becomes a real problem.

Tennis is a game of explosive action, punctuated by graceful and often delicate movements. The world's greatest players demonstrate awesome power in serving and smashing, but at the same time are capable of the most delicate drop shots.

On average, points consist of short five or six stroke rallies in which speed, agility and balance are essential, and a player without these qualities has very limited potential. Strength and power, particularly in the men's game, is important to produce the service ace or the devastating smash or volley – remember Kevin Curren's 33 aces which destroyed Jimmy Connors at Wimbledon. In women's tennis and in many clay court matches, players must often be prepared to rally from the back of the court and retrieve for up to 50 strokes. This involves continuous heavy activity for the length of time it might take an athlete to run 400 or 800 metres at full pace. Then you might have to do it again in the next rally! Bjorn Borg and many of the Swedish stars have shown how matches can be won by being able to sustain technique and concentration over long and arduous rallies – a tribute to their exceptional stamina.

The champions are the players who can call on all these fitness qualities when the occasion demands.It should be the aim of every player to ensure that where fitness is concerned they will not be found wanting.

body in such a way that it enables you to deal with the physical demands of the game. You are trying to create improvements in the working of the heart, lungs and general body circulation and of the muscles, tendons and joints. By causing these changes there will naturally be improvements in the components or elements of fitness.

Components such as stamina and muscle endurance may be developed within the tennis practice and game situation provided this is extensive and correctly structured, but to improve flexibility, strength (power), speed and agility significantly you need to undertake specific fitness work in addition to tennis training.

TRAINING ELEMENTS

What you are trying to do in fitness training is to improve the exercise efficiency of the

Element	Exercises
Flexibility The ability to move the body parts through a wide range of positions, e.g. stretching sideways for a low volley.	Stretching, flexing, mobility exercises involving all major muscle groups and joints.
Strength (power) The ability to exert great force, e.g. the punch in the winning volley or the devastating smash.	Heavy muscle work, explosive exercises. Weights (heavy, low repetitions 5–10).
Muscle endurance The ability to use individual groups of muscles for a sustained period, e.g. arm and shoulder muscles in a long service game.	Body resistance exercises, circuit training. Weights (light, high repetitions 10–20).
Stamina Continuous, strenuous body activity, e.g. maintaining quality performance without fatigue over a three-hour match.	Running: continuous, interval, shuttles, skipping, circuits. Aerobic and anaerobic training.
Speed The ability to move at great pace, e.g. sprinting from behind the baseline to the net to retrieve a drop shot.	Flexibility and strength exercises. Sprints: short and long (20–100 metres); continued speed and agility exercises.
Agility The ability to adjust position and change direction at great speed, e.g. picking up a drop shot and turning quickly to get back for a lob.	Flexibility exercises. Court related exercises: shuttles, circuits, twisting, turning, bouncing, skipping etc. Combine speed and agility exercises.

TRAINING PRINCIPLES

When planning your training schedules and programmes ensure that you use the following principles which are common to all sports.

Overload

Your fitness must be built up so that you can more than meet the demands of the game. This involves the principle of overload, which means that the body must be pushed beyond its normal limits and is therefore under unaccustomed pressure. This is where commitment and dedication are called for: it requires hard work and it can hurt. The rewards are an improvement in performance as the body adapts to the increased workload and can be pushed to further limits. The aim should be to train the system so that ultimately you reach the stage where the body never becomes overloaded in the game. As Sebastian Coe says: the race (match) should be a rest day (physically).

Progression

There must be a steady and continuous progression in fitness training. You must always aim for new peaks because there are no limits to fitness levels. Continue to overload systematically and never be satis-

Fig 87 Becker needs a superb level of fitness to play shots like these.

fied with your performance. This will enable you to work harder during the match and produce better and better performances.

Reversibility

If you stop training, you start to slide back – reversibility. You must therefore avoid training breaks if possible and continue to maintain quality work. Injury, illness or excessive tournament play often cause unavoidable problems, but peaks and troughs in performance are natural and once you have learned your capabilities it is much easier to build up again providing you are prepared to work hard. A break from training is sometimes psychologically sound as long as you are prepared for a renewed effort when you start again.

Specificity

All sportspeople require a general fitness programme, but each sport makes its own very specific demands. The requirements for a tennis player are quite different from those for a boxer and, more surprisingly, the squash or badminton player.

The tennis player who lacks speed and agility will always struggle, and training should be designed to develop these components to the maximum with exercises as close to the game situation as possible. Different types of players have different types of fitness requirements; the training for the serve and volley specialist (like Boris Becker) who thrives on speed and power will be different from the steady baseliner (like Mats Wilander) who needs greater stamina.

The principle of specificity therefore applies not only to the game of tennis as a whole but also to the needs of the individual player.

Measurement

It is a tremendous motivating factor when a player is able to recognise and appreciate improvements in his fitness and performance. It is important, therefore, to check your fitness levels throughout your training period and continue to set yourself a series of targets and goals.

A training diary is critical for checking progress. You should record brief details of your training programme and schedules on a daily, weekly and monthly basis and significant results of training sessions and fitness tests that you may give yourself. This will soon show you what considerable improvements can be made in your fitness levels and, ultimately, to your tennis performance.

Warm-up

No intensive fitness work or tennis game should commence until you have prepared your body thoroughly for action. This requires a gradual build-up of activity so that the body, particularly the muscles and joints, is eased into a condition where it is ready for the instant high-powered action which is part and parcel of tennis training and playing.

About 10 to 15 minutes should be devoted to the warm up and it should follow this simple plan:

1. Easy jogging for a minute or two to shake the muscles up generally and get the circulation going.
2. General stretching, flexing and mobility exercises of the muscles and joints which will be used during play and training.
3. More strenuous exercises, such as striding, high knee running, star-jumps, tuck-jumps and squat-jumps.

4. Movements which are closely related to the game situation with a gradual build-up to near maximum effort. This could be done on court with a racket.

5. Finish by feeling nice and loose, perspiring gently, only mildly fatigued and ready for action within one or two minutes.

Warm-down

After a strenuous work-out it is essential to wind down with some further loosening exercises and easy jogging to bring the body gradually back to normal and then immediately have a bath or shower. This will ward off the possibility of stiffness or soreness.

ORGANISATION

Tennis is now played all year round and it is possible for top players to be involved in almost continuous tournament play. Tennis practice, coaching and fitness training must therefore be carefully planned to fit in with competition commitments. There is a grave danger, however, particularly with younger players, that they enter too many tournaments for which they are often ill-prepared both technically and physically. Perhaps there is a need to play fewer tournaments and thus allow for a more constructive and measured preparation which would naturally give better results.

In the end, though, competition is the essence of the game, and training, both technical and physical, must be built around *important* match play – hence the need for very careful planning.

Unless you are very fortunate and have your own personal coach to make all your plans, or you are able to attend regular training and coaching sessions at your club, county, regional or national centre, you will be in control of your own destiny as far as organising your training programme is concerned. This proves to be too much for some players as tennis training can be a lonely occupation requiring tremendous commitment, patience, mental and physical effort and sound organisation, and only the most dedicated will realise their potential.

Look carefully at the time and facilities you have at your disposal before embarking on over-elaborate and unrealistic schemes. You need a simple running and exercising area – a tennis court or playing field will do – and if you have a running track, gymnasium (with weights) or any other indoor area, these are bonuses.

Training Time

For older aspiring juniors and regular tournament players.

Number of days	3–5
Number of hours	Minimum of 3 per week
Number of sessions	3 × 1 hour
	4 × 45 minutes
	5 × 30–40 minutes

Substitute extra fitness sessions if no tennis time is available.

Now take note of the following major points when organising your programme.

General

1. Plan a daily, weekly, monthly and yearly programme.

2. Record timetables, schedules, results, performances and so on in your training diary.

Fig 88 Martina Navratilova, demonstrating the need for suppleness,
agility and all-round fitness.

3. Establish a regular training routine — form good habits.

4. Plan carefully in relation to your competition commitments and avoid new or extra-strenuous schedules just before competition (allow at least 24 hours of rest).

Special

1. For progression, try to train each fitness element the equivalent of twice per week.

2. Organise extra sessions to develop major weaknesses, for example strength.

3. Always perform speed and agility sessions before heavy strength, endurance or skills sessions.

4. Never perform heavy strength or endurance sessions before skills sessions unless adequate rest of between two and three hours has been allowed.

5. Training prior to competition (on the day or 24 hours before) should be limited to light intensity work: flexibility, speed or aerobic exercises.

If you intend to reach your maximum potential, training has to become a year round habit. Get your diary out now and construct a plan of campaign, taking advice from experienced coaches, players and other experts. It will pay handsome dividends.

For further information and full details of tennis specific training schedules see *Fit for Tennis* by Bev Risman (Batsfords Ltd).

9 The Mental Game

The previous chapters have largely been concerned with the application of tennis skills, but there are many sports psychologists who have written as much and more about the mental activity and the part it plays in the competitive life of sportsmen. This chapter is a small contribution to this field to make you aware of its importance in match play. The comments are of a general nature, concerning things that happen to anyone who plays competitively at any level of the game, but it must be understood that each player is an individual character, whose attitudes and approach to the game may be completely different from the next player's.

Human nature dictates that tennis matches always involve some nervous tension. The more important the occasion, the greater will be the build-up of psychological pressures. How you handle these pressures will have a bearing on your future standard of play.

PSYCHOLOGICAL FACTORS

Nervous Tension

Stress and pressure are an infinite part of match play, together with *fear* – fear of losing a match you desperately want to win; fear of missing a shot; fear of playing badly in an important match.

Let's look at an extremely common example. You are playing against a known higher ranked opponent; having won the first set and leading 5–3 with your serve to follow, you are hit with the realisation that you are on the verge of a great win. Then the fear of losing the match begins to interfere; a nervous service game may follow, the nervousness creating tension in the muscles which can affect the technical quality of your strokes. Unless it can be overcome, that fear of losing may become a reality.

If you are going to play the game to any reasonable level, nervous tension must be kept under control to some degree. A practical way of helping to lower your level of anxiety is to practise developing a sound technique in match-like situations that you know you will be able to trust in a real match.

Relaxation

Relaxation and the ability to control pre-match tension can be the best way of ensuring that you give of your best. Players who are playing in their first final or who have been selected for a team for the first time are probably the most vulnerable to pre-match tension. Although they have worked hard for these moments of recognition, the excitement of it all could work against them. Too much excitement could have them rushing around in the match, their match strategy and tactics forgotten. A player must develop ways of calming that excitement down before the event.

Many good players, however, believe that the nervous excitement they feel is good for them if they are to play well. The nervous element disappears quickly when the match is under way, only the excitement remains. Excitement for them is a natural symptom; they have been in this situation before.

Players in all sports have their own ways of lowering these pre-match tensions. Some favour the thoughts of happy things as a means of quietening the mind. Remembering pleasant and happy experiences can help you to relax for play; but you do have to practise the art of doing it. Others like to find a quiet spot, then play their matches in their imagination, *always winning* the big points, the important games and the match: seeing their best shots flowing down the court, retrieving their opponent's best shots, and turning difficult situations into match-winning moves.

Reading is another method favoured by many. Tom Watson, the great American golfer, studies car mechanic books to quieten his excitement down and only lets his mind dwell on the important round of golf ahead when he begins to dress for play. Listening to favourite music seems to be another way of lowering tension, its soothing effect is easily imagined.

Goal Setting

You want to win; but to win what? It could be one particular match or one particular tournament. Some may want to win the respect of other players and spectators by playing well, even though they may lose the match.

Winning can be simply setting yourself certain goals and achieving them. The goals you set can be:

1. Long term targets to achieve by a given time in the future.

2. Short term targets that are stepping-stones towards the happy ending you have predicted for yourself.

It is important to set yourself goals that are demanding but reachable. This way you will gain in self-confidence and look forward to attaining each new goal in turn.

The following example shows how easy it is to focus on the long term and fall short of success. The long term for this player was to reach the final of a major championship and confront once again the opponent who had beaten him in the final the previous year. He had been concentrating all his efforts towards this match, but lost in the semi-final to a player he should have beaten. He was beaten precisely because he was unable to focus attention on the short term task. He had been looking too far ahead.

Henri Leconte made this comment, with a huge smile, after losing to Boris Becker in the 1986 Wimbledon semi-final: 'I lost to him last year in the quarter-finals, this year it's the semi-finals, maybe next year I will lose to him in the final and the year after that maybe I will beat him in the final.' Is this Leconte's long term goal? I am sure it is. But I am equally sure he is now concentrating on the short term goals.

Positive Thinking

Winning is not your right, it must be earned. 'I will win this next match' may be a positive approach, but it only makes sense when the player has also prepared correctly for the match. Taking nothing for granted, he has put in a sensible practice period, studied his opponent in play, and formed a plan of campaign. This must include the overall strategy he intends to use and the tactics he must use to bring it all to a

Fig 89   Nervous tension, when controlled, can enhance a player's game.

uccessful conclusion.

A player's positive thinking is based on his willingness to prepare and leave nothing to chance, well aware that there are two players vying for the win. A good opponent will surely make it as difficult as possible for you, and after all the hours of practice, a great deal of thinking and pre-match preparation you must go out there and prove you can win.

Enjoy the Challenge

Enjoying competition is certainly more likely to bring you a frequent visit to the winner's enclosure. If you look forward to matches the tensions and pressures we talked about earlier may be easier to control.

Some players you see in matches don't run and chase balls, they are not interested in retrieving their opponent's best shots and they believe their own good shots should never be returned. Luck always appears against them, but in fact they haven't developed the right attitude for successful competition.

Learn from your Defeats

You should never be frightened of losing; it is always a possibility. If you have practised, prepared well, done all you could to win and still lost, you may, after the initial disappointment, admit that your opponent was the better player on the day. That in itself is *positive thinking*, and from that point you will begin to re-evaluate your performance and use this information to prepare for your next match. You may have to suffer the same disappointment many times, but if you continue to assess realistically the

matches you lose, you will surely begin to win more matches.

Above a doorway between the dressing-rooms and the centre court at Wimbledon are these words written by Rudyard Kipling: 'If you can meet with triumph and disaster and treat these two imposters both the same'. Some of the world's best players after walking through the doors have experienced what may have seemed to them a disaster and returned another year for the triumph. If you enjoy the thrills of competition, you too can learn from your defeats and be better prepared for the subsequent triumphs.

SUMMARY

As a player approaches the advanced level, it should no longer be necessary for him to think consciously of the details of his stroke technique, which has been perfected by disciplined practice. Now he has the attitude of a cool, concentrated winner, with his nerves under control, trusting himself and his ability, thinking only of the necessary tactics to win, confident of overcoming any unexpected eventuality and knowing he can outlast his opponent physically and mentally. He is a winner, possibly a champion.

For the rest of us, try to be realistic and honest about your game, its strengths and its weaknesses. Reduce the latter by efficient practice sessions, without forgetting to practise the strengths. Make a strong commitment through a love of the game. In anything in life, a determined will to succeed is a sure recipe for success.

10 The Practical Game

In the previous chapters we have looked in detail at many aspects of tennis which, if studied and put into practice, can help to improve your techniques, tactics, fitness, mental attitude and, finally, your overall game. In this chapter we shall look at the practical aspects of clubs, coaching and competition.

Anyone who enjoys playing tennis should try to play as frequently as possible. How often you play depends almost entirely on your reasons for playing and your level of aspiration. The social players who play purely for fun, enjoy meeting new friends and are not interested in competitive play outside a small circle of friends, might well enjoy playing just once or twice a week or even less. They can still achieve a tremendous amount of satisfaction and fun by simply playing a social level of tennis. On the other hand, committed, competitive players, who want to improve and compete at a higher level, would probably play three or four times a week with a high level of commitment to practising and competing.

CLUBS

Both the social player and the competitive player are looking for satisfaction and fulfilment at their own levels, and it is therefore important for them to choose carefully the type of club where they will play their tennis.

The social player should look for opportunities to play with similar friends, hopefully on a regular basis. The opportunities for social players may lie in a private members club which has organised club nights, social evenings and a desire to help its membership meet and have fun whilst playing tennis. This player could also get satisfaction and enjoyment from clubs organised by the local authorities in the parks or in their leisure centres. It is also possible to organise your own tennis by hiring court facilities at the parks and leisure centres.

If, however, you are a committed tennis player, you will obviously be looking for a different set of opportunities. Hopefully you will still be looking for the fun and the social interaction that tennis can provide, but you will also be looking for more in the way of competition and matches. You will require a club with a membership that has keen tennis players who wish to improve and who will be regularly available.

To get your full enjoyment and satisfaction, whichever type of player you are, it is important for you to assess the opportunities that the club offers you. The well-balanced club will offer regular play for its membership, including both singles and doubles. It will have social tennis with club nights which give the members a chance to meet new friends. It will have a variety of internal tournaments including ladders, leagues, one-day tournaments and so on. It will have club teams who will represent the club in competitions and leagues, and it will organise coaching sessions for its members.

If you wish to join a club, it is advisable to find out its full range of activities before joining. Remember, a club should service the needs of all its members. There are over 2,500 Lawn Tennis Association affiliated tennis clubs in Great Britain, plus many new purpose-built indoor tennis centres where you can play and enjoy your tennis all the year round. If you are not already a member, why not join now?

COACHING

You may think it a surprising question, but many people ask from time to time what the benefits are of having coaching. To anyone playing tennis, whatever their standard and commitment, tremendous benefits can be gained by having coaching from a qualified coach.

The social tennis player will find that a course of lessons, whether individual or in a small group, will be geared to helping them enjoy the game more. The coach will not try to turn them into world beaters but will try to raise their level of performance with simple tips and by increasing their understanding of not only the technical and tactical aspects of tennis, but also the practical side. This will enable the social player to have far greater enjoyment in the game of tennis and develop self-confidence which will enable them to increase their circle of friends and players.

The committed tennis player will be looking for a different level of coaching, as he wishes to improve his standard in order to compete more successfully. The coach will assess his pupil's standard and ambition and will then tailor a programme which will be specifically geared towards helping him improve. Many people think a coach will only work on a player's technique. This is a fallacy, although the coach may find in many instances that faulty technique is stopping the player from developing his true potential. However, the successful coach evaluates the player's strengths and weaknesses not only in the technical side of his game, but also in the tactical, physical and psychological side. The coach will then discuss with the player the areas of improvement necessary (remembering that a coach does not just eradicate weakness but also improves strengths). He will then, in conjunction with the player, formulate a course of action that will not only help the player improve specific parts of his game, but also increase his knowledge and awareness of what he is trying to do within that game.

Coaches and players should be a partnership, with the coach dispensing knowledge and the player acquiring a greater understanding of all aspects of tennis whilst improving his game. That is not the end of the story, however. The coach will also advise the player on equipment, competitions, tournaments and standards required for competing at a higher level. It could be said that a coach should be all things to all people.

The Lawn Tennis Association Training of Coaches Scheme has three levels of qualified teachers and coaches:

1. Elementary Tennis Teacher – who is qualified to teach all ages at the beginner level.
2. Assistant Coach – who is qualified to teach up to junior county standard and senior club league standard.
3. Professional Coach – who is qualified to teach at all levels and ages from the beginner up to county and national standard.

If you wish to ensure you receive the correct coaching/teaching standards, check that your teacher/coach has the appropriate qualification.

Coaching Opportunities

The Lawn Tennis Association is instrumental in organising three tiers of coaching and training for the country's most talented and promising players:

1. County Coaching and Training organised by the appropriate County Lawn Tennis Association.
2. Regional Coaching and Training organised by the appropriate LTA region and administered by the National Coach/ Development Officer in the region.
3. National Training organised by the LTA National Training Department based mainly at Bisham Abbey, the LTA National Training Centre.

All three tiers offer assisted or scholarship training to the most talented players, as well as competitions, representative matches and other opportunities. The LTA also organises and administers Starter Tennis Courses throughout the country, giving thousands of young players their first opportunity to play and receive instruction in tennis.

Coaches' Associations

The Professional Tennis Coaches' Association of Great Britain is an Association formed of LTA Professional Coaches and LTA Assistant Coaches. The aims of the Association are to increase the standard of its membership in all coaching matters and provide a body of expertise that will help to raise the standards of coaches, coaching and players throughout the country.

The County Coaches' Association has

the same aims and objectives as the Professional Tennis Coaches' Association, but draw their membership from either one county or one region. The membership in general comprises all three levels of LTA coach, and in some Associations anyone with an interest in tennis may join.

The Club Coach

The Club Coach is generally qualified to LTA Assistant Coach or LTA Professional Coach level. His job is to provide the club with a well-balanced coaching programme for all ages and all standards. This will range from Short Tennis courses, Junior Beginner courses, Adult Starter courses, individual lessons for all standards, team training plus organising competitions, social tennis, club nights, American tournaments, film shows, and so on, all of which are designed to help the member in their tennis development.

The modern tennis coach is no longer the coach who gives individual lessons all day. He is very often a major influence overall in the developments of the tennis club.

If you want to improve, you will find the coach can help you in many different ways

COMPETITIONS

Now you have finally reached the area of tennis that interests almost everyone. Many social players will feel that competition is not for them, but in reality they are wrong. The very moment anyone steps on to the tennis court and hits balls against another person, they are, in effect, competing. It may be at a very elementary level and purely for fun, but nevertheless this is the beginning of competition. Where it goes from there depends on how much enjoy ment the player gets from competition and whether or not they wish to test their abilities at a higher level. There is no doubt that you will always get out of competition what you put into it.

The early stages of competition can sometimes be frustrating if you do not set yourself sensible goals. There is no disgrace in entering a competition and being beaten, because in any match there must always be a winner and a loser. If you can evaluate your opponent's standard, you may find that he is a far superior player. In this situation, set yourself a reasonable target – possibly to win four games each set, or even to win a set. Should you succeed in doing this, you could possibly have achieved a personal best and, although losing, you may well have played better than ever before.

So remember, in competition set yourself attainable goals which, if achieved, become a win in themselves.

Types of Competition

There are many different forms of competition both individual and team. The following are a selection.

Club Ladders

Players are placed on a ladder in the club in order of merit, number one being the best and the highest number being the least experienced. They are allowed to challenge approximately three places above and, if they win, they go into the position above the player they have just beaten and everybody else on the ladder goes down a place. This is a very good system for players to find their level of performance.

Club Leagues

These are similar in concept to a ladder, with all players starting off in leagues in approximate order of merit. Generally, five or six players play in a league with each player playing against each other member of the league. At the end of a set period of time, approximately three or four weeks, the league is complete with players in order of merit, generally one to five. The winner is promoted to the league above and the bottom player is relegated to the league below. The league then recommences for the next period.

Knock-out Tournaments

These are tournaments where, if there are 32 players in a draw, the 32 players are paired off into 16 matches for round one. After round one, there are 16 players who are winners who go into round two. They are paired off into eight matches to produce eight winners for round three and so on until there is a final winner. The first round losers will play one match, the second round losers will play two matches, and so on, and this is why it is called a knock-out tournament.

American Tournament

In American tournaments everybody plays everybody else and the winner is the one with the most number of points. The points score will be two for a win and one for a draw. In an American tournament of eight people, everybody will play seven matches and there will be a total of 28 matches played altogether. At the end of the American tournament it is possible to make a ranking list of players based upon the final results table.

Fig 90   Boris Becker enjoying the triumph of his Wimbledon win in 1985.

Fig 91   Tennis has no place for bad sports: Becker and Leconte, after a
hard match, still sportsmen and friends.

Round Robin Tournament

These are similar to American tournaments and are often used when the numbers in an American tournament become too many. For example, with 24 players there are four separate groups of six. Each group will play an American tournament amongst its group members which will result in four winners. The winners will then either go into another group round robin to find the winner or into a knock-out competition. It is possible with the round robin tournament to emerge with a full order of merit of all participants.

Postal Tournaments

Postal tournaments are tournaments where there is no central venue for each match. Players are drawn to play other matches on either a home or away basis. The home player arranges the venue, balls and so on, and the away player has to travel to the home player's choice of venue. The result of the match is posted to the organiser who informs the winners of the responsibilities for the next round of matches, and so on.

Ratings Tournament

The ratings tournament has recently been introduced to Great Britain. The intention is to provide a tournament where players of similar standard are drawn together in groups to compete against each other in the initial stages. The winners of a section receive prizes and qualify for the next stages of the tournament amongst the higher rating players. The tournament

The Practical Game

generally lasts two weeks at one venue and each rating section is completed in approximately three to four days. At the end of the first section, the winners are qualified to go through to compete in the higher rating section over the next three to four days. When this rating section is completed, the winners again go through. The top rated players do not enter the competition until the last three days, whilst everyone else is playing through to meet them.

A player's rating will govern which section of the draw he is placed into. The player's initial rating will be ascertained by the information supplied. Players may be re-rated during the season at any time if they have been placed in a section that is not suitable to their standard.

There are well over 200 ratings tournaments per year in Great Britain and all the information is centralised on computer to facilitate the organisation and evaluation of players' ratings. This is a tremendous boost for the keen competitive player who may now enter tournaments knowing that he has a chance to compete regularly and in a planned way. These undoubtedly will raise the standard of competition enormously over the next decade.

Closed Tournaments

These are tournaments that are 'closed' to a certain category of membership. For example, a club closed tournament will only accept competitors from its membership and not from outsiders. The closed tournament can take varied forms, for example knock-out, round robin and so on.

Open Tournaments

This is a tournament open to all players. It has no restrictions and it is possible that a novice may play a national player in the first round. The competition can again take various forms.

Satellite Tournament

These are a series of tournaments run by the governing body for players who are trying to become full-time professional tennis players and who wish to break into the Grand Prix tennis circuit.

There are qualifying tournaments for the satellite competitions. The most successful players in the satellite generally earn computer points which may qualify them for direct entry into Grand Prix tournaments, ATP (Association of Tennis Professionals) and WITA (Women's International Tennis Association) tournaments.

Team Competition

The team members normally represent the club in singles or doubles, in league competitions or in knock-out competitions. The competitions may include county league up to national knock-out competitions and national league competitions.

County Competitions

Players are chosen to represent their county in singles, doubles, inter-county leagues and knock-out competitions.

Regional Competitions

These are for juniors up to 18. The players are chosen to represent their region in competitions and representative matches.

International Teams

These represent their country in individual and team competitions, for example for ladies – the Wightman Cup and the Federation Cup, and for men – the European Cup and the Davis Cup.

As you can see, there is a full range of competitive opportunities available for all levels of player. We hope that you will find your level of competition and, hopefully, be able to improve it.

SUMMARY

To play tennis well requires considerable skill, and to acquire these skills it is necessary to have a sound understanding of the areas covered in the previous chapters. To be successful at any level requires time and patience and, as with any other sport, to reach the top the player's level of commitment must be high. Time and enthusiasm must be spent in learning and practising new techniques and skills. Results will come with the knowledge that progress cannot be rushed as there is no guaranteed time-scale for improvement. Sometimes improvement shows almost overnight, other times it can take weeks or even months. To be a successful tennis player you must be willing to keep working and practising all the time.

The ideas and skills depicted in this book will help you to increase your knowledge of the skills of tennis and, hopefully, gain more satisfaction from your increased level of performance.

The chances are that, given all the right ingredients, you too could become a top player, even a champion. But do not be disheartened if, like the majority of us, you play only to average level. The important thing is that you should have fun, enjoyment and friendship from this marvellous game of tennis which can be truly called '*a game for a lifetime*'.

Useful Addresses

The Lawn Tennis Association
Queens Club
West Kensington
London W14 9EG

The Lawn Tennis Foundation, British Tennis Umpires' Association, British Schools' LTA and the LTA Regional Offices can all be contacted at the above address.

Professional Tennis Coaches' Association
21A Glencairn Court
Lansdowne Road
Cheltenham
Gloucestershire

International Tennis Federation
1 Palliser Road
West Kensington
London W14

National Coaching Foundation
4 College Close
Beckett Park
Leeds
North Yorkshire

The Scottish Lawn Tennis Association
12 Melville Crescent
Edinburgh EH3 7LU

The Welsh Lawn Tennis Association
National Sports Centre for Wales
Sophia Gardens
Cardiff

Index

Crowood Sports Books

American Football – The Skills of the Game	*Les Wilson*
Badminton – The Skills of the Game	*Peter Roper*
Basketball – The Skills of the Game	*Paul Stimpson*
Canoeing – Skills and Techniques	*Neil Shave*
The Skills of Cricket	*Keith Andrew*
Crown Green Bowls – The Skills of the Game	*Harry Barratt*
Endurance Running	*Norman Brook*
Fitness for Sport	*Rex Hazeldine*
Golf – The Skills of the Game	*John Stirling*
Hockey – The Skills of the Game	*John Cadman*
Judo – Skills and Techniques	*Tony Reay*
Jumping	*Malcolm Arnold*
Karate – The Skills of the Game	*Vic Charles*
Rugby Union – The Skills of the Game	*Barrie Corless*
Skiing – Developing Your Skill	*John Shedden*
Cross-Country Skiing	*Paddy Field and Tim Walker*
Sprinting and Hurdling	*Peter Warden*
Squash – The Skills of the Game	*Ian McKenzie*
Swimming	*John Verrier*
Table Tennis – The Skills of the Game	*Gordon Steggall*
Tennis – The Skills of the Game	*Charles Applewhaite and Bill Moss*
Throwing	*Max Jones*
Volleyball – The Skills of the Game	*Keith Nicholls*
Windsurfing – Improving Techniques	*Ben Oakley*